The WEALTH flow CODE

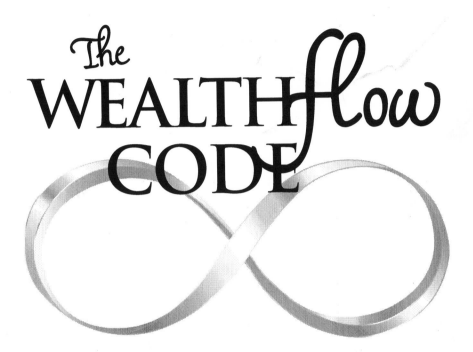

FINDING FOCUS, FREEDOM AND BALANCE IN A HIGH-STRESS CAREER

Julianne Joy

Praise

"The WealthFlow Code *is well-organized and practical. It offers a great introduction to anyone who's had difficulty creating or maintaining, emotional or physical balance. Julianne provides clear and straightforward information, and most importantly, a simple set of steps and helpful tools to guide one towards greater well-being."*

—Marcia Formica, author, blogger,
food sustainability evangelist

"In a world so out of balance, it's refreshing to find a book that hits the restart button! The WealthFlow Code *offers so many healthy tips for optimal wellness of body, mind and spirit. A must read!"*

—Windy Cook, M.S.W, author of *Sisterhood of the Mindful Goddess*

"The WealthFlow Code *is written from the heart in easy to read steps that I've already begun to put into daily practice. I am looking forward to living my life in new ways! Thank you Julianne for sharing your experience, knowledge, and wisdom."*

—Barbara Taylor-Hatje

"Julianne's writing style makes TheWealthFlow Code *so easy to read, easy to understand, and easy to follow! I appreciate the references to other sources and studies that back up her philosophy and practices. This book is a manual for pursuing a better life that the reader can actually understand and apply. I learned so much about the principles of meditation, connecting with nature, and nutrition for mental, emotional, and physical well-being. I am now paying attention to my circadian rhythms and am more aware of how my own energy flow can help me be more productive. Thank you for the Focus Keeper App. A very well-written, insightful book!"*

—Jill Kovalich, President, JMK MarComm LLC

"In TheWealthFlow Code, *Julianne Joy weaves both her own and others' wisdom to offer the reader an accessible and practical guide to an empowered life. This book provides a good starting place for those new to meditation and somatic work."*

—Wendy Shumway

"In The WealthFlow Code, *Julianne Joy shares how to bridge our inner and outer worlds to experience wellness. This doesn't happen by reading books, it happens by doing the work, putting in the time, and incorporating all that you have experienced and learned into finding and being in your flow. Health is the new currency, and Julianne's philosophy of tapping into frequencies of energy and using alternative approaches to traditional healing modalities is the best way to optimize wellness."*

—Debbie Sodergren, energy body vibration expert, author of *Just Be...a mindful way to love your life.*

FLOWER *of* LIFE PRESS™

The WealthFlow™ Code: Finding Focus, Freedom, and Balance in a High-Stress Career
By Julianne Joy

The content of this book is for general instruction only. Each person's physical, emotional, and spiritual condition is unique. The instruction in this book is not intended to replace or interrupt the reader's relationship with a physician or other mental health professional. Please consult your doctor for matters pertaining to your specific health.

Book design and cover by Astara Jane Ashley, **www.floweroflifepress.com**

To contact the author, visit **www.juliannejoy.me**

Published by Flower of Life Press, *Old Saybrook, CT.*
To contact the publisher, visit **www.floweroflifepress.com**
Download your FREE GIFT: **www.bestsellerpriestess.com/bestseller-priestess**

Library of Congress Control Number: 2019912117

ISBN-13: 978-1-7337409-5-1

Printed in the United States of America

Dedication

I would like to dedicate this book to all my friends, family, and mentors who have tirelessly supported me along my journey (which seemed like an eternity to me) as I took the steps along my path to find focus, freedom, and balance through experiences of writing, journaling, adventure, *fun*, and *joy*—along with many trials and tribulations.

Special thanks to my sons, Brendan and Bryan, for loving me unconditionally, even when I worked so much that I didn't spend as much time with them as I would have liked to because I didn't have these tools to create work-life balance when they were growing up.

Thank you to Ed and his family for their love and support during this transition period in my life.

I also dedicate this to my loving parents, and my sister and her wildly creative children Samantha and Cassandra, as well as my brother and his son Nathaniel who have been great sounding boards along my journey.

And of course, to all of the mentors and friends who have facilitated my growth over the last few years. My wish is that this book will help free others from the mindset traps that I was entrenched in for so many years of my life. There truly is a better way.

Contents

Prologue

Initially this book was going to be released in 2019, but now, on July of 2020, I can see in hindsight that everything happens in perfect timing.

Living in these times of the pandemic Covid-19 means that more and more people are suffering, and are also asking for help! They need the tools in this book now more than ever because of the added social isolation, stress and anxiety that we are all now dealing with, such as adjusting to working from home, the lack of socialization that we used to get at the office, juggling work with home schooling, and the added layers of fears around health and safety, and access to food and toiletries.

For me, the pandemic has brought in a great deal of self-reflection and shined a light on how I am living my life and what is really important to me.

This book is a playbook to create a better life by using the powerful techniques and tools inside as you create a consistent self-care practice.

Introduction

My Body Meltdown

One morning during tax season of 2016, I finally had the deep realization that if I didn't listen to what my body was trying to tell me, then I'd be facing extremely severe consequences. I'd been working long hours every day for at least six—if not seven—days a week, in an attempt to meet all of my deadlines as a tax accountant. But now, my body was bleeding, I was exhausted, and I was completely run down.

Something was wrong.

I felt like I was about to cry at any moment and was at the end of my rope with the stress. My chest felt constricted, making it very difficult to even take a breath. The ton of bricks on my shoulders was weighing me down so much that I could barely get up.

There was twisting, searing pain in my bladder—it felt like someone was stabbing me with a knife! But I just kept saying to myself, "Just one more tax return...just a few more days and then I can stop...I need to make my deadlines!"

However, my body had other plans. I finally gave in and called the doctor. Because I had ignored the earlier signs, I ended up having to go for several tests at the hospital and was given antibiotics. But when the medication didn't work, I ended up with an even stronger prescription. Finally, one day, I heard the message loud and clear in my mind: *Take care of yourself or be taken out!*

Learning to Listen

My body's meltdown was a *huge* wake-up call for me to re-prioritize my health and take better care of myself. I knew that something was wrong, I just needed to listen and take appropriate action. So after much trial and error with various modalities and protocols, I developed the WealthFlow Code 7-step process for bringing the body back into balance. By following these steps, I was able to get through the next two consecutive tax seasons unscathed and am now grateful to be sharing these tools so other people can avoid the suffering I went through. I experienced so much stress during tax season that I could barely breathe!

I had to learn the hard way, and I *really* don't want you to have to do the same. If you're like me, suffering has been a way of life, and now it's time to change the rules so you no longer have to struggle so much. Struggling is *optional,* and if I can change, you can too!

You can start by shifting your thinking and practice listening to the cues your body is giving you. Listening allows you to tap into the sacred intelligence that lives in your body. It's time to say goodbye to being a victim and take radical responsibility for your health. When you listen to your body, you will be able to avoid illness. You can be your own hero! But first, in order to change your life, there are a few requirements:

- Be present in each moment and learn to silence your mind chatter.
- Find a state of peace and serenity through proper breathing.
- Trust in and surrender to the innate wisdom of your body.
- Take action in order to change and create what you really desire in your life and health.

We're all made of energy, and to achieve optimal balance, it's vitally important to not only address the physical and emotional aspects of your well-being, but to balance, maintain, and protect your energy.

Start to pay attention to your thoughts, because where your attention goes, your energy flows. It's too easy to leak energy when one is telling the same stories of negativity and struggle over and over again.

When you follow the guidance in this book, you will awaken to more positivity and a better way of managing your stress, and then you'll be able to choose to avoid the negative side effects of a high-stress career altogether!

By simply listening to your body, you will be able to adjust your routine and incorporate the tools that you need before it is too late. In my case, I wasn't listening to my body and didn't have the necessary steps in place to prevent illness and maintain my energy, so I went through a healing crisis. I had no choice but to figure out how to heal myself. And, if I had not listened to my body when I did, it could have been disastrous!

But you do not have to wait for your body to fall apart to make the changes you desire. Let's take a look at what energy is, and some of the important tools you'll be using through the WealthFlow Code 7-step process.

Awakening to the Power of Energy

"You can choose where you put the energy of your attention.
Energy flows where attention goes."
—Robert Moss

When you tap into the power of your own energetic body, you'll begin to notice synchronicities in your life that will seem almost magical! For instance, have you ever thought about someone right as your phone rang and it was them on the other line? This happened to me recently. As I was sipping my morning tea, I was thinking about my brother and how grateful I was for the mug he gifted me. Right as I was radiating with gratitude for him, my phone rang—*and it was him*!

Think of energy as everything we *can't* normally see around us. In order to truly transform, you need to understand a few things about these "unseen" realms. First, as vibrational beings, we are all made of vibrating particles. In fact, our entire Universe is made of these vibrating particles of energy!

Every thought has a waveform, just like a microwave or radio signal. The energy you send out into the universe via your thoughts attracts the same energy back to you. Quantum physics is the science behind this: it shows us that once you activate a particular vibration such as joy in your being, you attract that same vibration back to you. You are the antenna attracting a particular vibrational frequency, just like an antenna receives a radio frequency. This is why we need to be mindful of where we focus our attention. If we focus on negativity, we attract more negativity into our lives. On the contrary, focusing on positivity allows us to attract more positivity into our lives. In fact, *every thought in your mind vibrates at its own frequency* and has an impact on your life and on the world. This is why it is so important to *be intentional with your thoughts*. What you focus on in your inner world of thoughts and feelings expands and creates your reality in the outer physical world. When you add intentional emotions and actions to your positive thoughts, they are activated to vibrate on a more powerful level.

> *"The greatest weapon against stress is our ability to choose one thought over another."*
>
> —William James

The Chakras

Your being consists of a physical body, an emotional body, and an energy body. Your energy body contains the chakras. In yoga, meditation, and Ayurveda, *chakra* is the Sanskrit term for "wheel" and refers to these energy centers found in the body.

The seven major energy centers in your body run from the base of your spine up to the crown of your head. Each chakra has its own color and location in the body, and the activity of each one is affected by your mental and emotional state, which is why daily stress can create chakra imbalances resulting in physical, physiological, or psychological disorders. When your chakras are balanced, you will feel maximum vitality and can get into a *flow* state. (Hint: *This is how we can get more done with less effort.*)

Chakra balancing is the process of restoring a harmonious flow of energy across your chakra system. When your chakras are balanced, you will feel more relaxed, centered, grounded, energized, and aware. By using specific tools, you can balance your chakras and increase your life force energy. For example, you can wear a specific color, eat specific foods, use essential oils, do yoga poses, or use musical notes to bring your chakras into balance. We'll explore the many ways to work with the chakras in everyday life to bring us into a flow state.

Once I discovered the presence of the chakras, I was able to change my life. Each of the following chapters will refer to one of the chakras and explain how it works.

Essential Oils

Essential oils (see *Resources* on page 111) are a wonderful tool to raise your vibration and uplift your energy. In the following chapters, I'll recommend several essential oils to help support you with each chakra. You can also use them in the office on a daily basis to support you with stress and overwhelm.

Before traveling on a recent business trip across the country, I filled small portable vials with the oils that I expected to use while I was away. I used peppermint essential oil to minimize jet lag from the time change. *I felt so supported!*

When I arrived at my location, I couldn't breathe because of sinus congestion, so I pulled out my doTERRA® *Breathe* oil which helps clear the airways. I used *Lemon* oil in my water daily to cleanse my body. I used *Deep Blue* essential oil for meditating, and *OnGuard* essential oil for low energy and to keep my immune system strong. I brought my travel diffuser and the *Lavender* oil helped me sleep at night. I also used an essential oil blend called *DigestZen* to help my belly when it didn't feel well after eating something that didn't agree with me. It was better than having a first aid kit, right at my fingertips! You can also diffuse essential oils or combine them with fractionated coconut oil, for example, to make a blend. It is a fun tool that you can *play* with!

The Universal Laws

Each step of the WealthFlow Code also utilizes the Laws of Nature, or Universal Laws. These are the principles that govern every aspect of the universe and are the means by which our world and the entire cosmos continues to exist, thrive and expand.

When you understand the universal laws and choose to consciously align with them, *your life will become easier* because you will be supported not only by others, but by the universe as well. You will flow with life more easily and be grateful for each event or circumstance you encounter as your life unfolds—no matter what your mind "thinks" it should be like!

Many people believe that life simply happens *to* them instead of *for* them. They'll perceive events as random and believe that there is no definitive purpose or underlying reason why things happen the way they do. But real transformation requires *trust* that there is a purpose and divine plan that is bigger than our small minds can conceive of.

Working with energy and the universal laws requires this trust and belief. A doubting mind is negative, and will only attract the same, thus stopping the potential flow and healing that you are looking for.

In order to work with the universal laws, you must first create a focused intention for *what* you desire. Then you will visualize it and focus on its realness as if it already exists *(feel into it with emotion)*. Ask for it and think, speak and act as if you already have it *(act as if)*. Then, take inspired action to make it a tangible reality and bring it into the here and now. Allow it to enter your life. Lastly, detach, trust, and surrender in order to receive the desired results. Receive it and be thankful for it.

Your only job is to define *what you desire* and *why* you desire it. The Universe will take care of *when* and *how it shows up*. The more intentional, focused, and consistent you are in defining what and why you want something, the faster the Universe will respond and you'll see it reflected back in your life.

When you don't align yourself with the Universal Laws, it's easy to stay stuck in the chase for "more". But after you align with the laws, you'll likely feel yourself wanting to simplify. You may discover that you want to release all the stuff you've accumulated and work less so that you can actually *live* more.

It's not about living to work,
it's about working to live.

We each have all the answers inside of us. But when you look outside of yourself for answers, your life is then dictated by external experiences that define your future and how your life unfolds. This is NOT conscious creation and YOU living life—rather it's life living YOU. It can result in severe imbalance resulting in exhaustion, overwhelm, depression, fear, and anxiety—the opposite of what we want! When we are in this lower vibration, we are blind to the *unlimited infinite abundance that is readily available to us in every moment.*

With the WealthFlow Code, you'll create more balance, focus, and freedom in your life. Your work life will rise to a whole new level and you'll begin to feel true success and aliveness. By following the practices in this book, you'll learn to remain calm, cool, and collected even in the midst of chaos. You'll learn to love your work life and see it as sacred.

So let's get to it and begin this process of saying goodbye to high stress and hello to a better work life!

Journal Entry – November 7, 2017

Yesterday I practiced my 'WealthFlow Code 7-step process' and the day felt like it lasted forever! I had so much time to do everything I needed to do, and I even went for a walk outside at 3 p.m. It was so warm out. I felt like a child at play and even saw some girls walking home from school who were singing together. It lifted my mood instantly and I was so relaxed and happy when I returned to my desk.

Just Breathe

Death by 1000 cuts

I recently had lunch with a business acquaintance. She told me a story about how her previous job was very stressful. She used the term "Death by 1,000 Cuts" and then she explained this concept to me. Stress can come in many shapes and forms. It can be one event that happens in one fell swoop, or it can be a failure that results from many small problems, which was her situation.

Stress can feel like a slow, lingering death process that acts like a form of torture, where you are hit by many small stressors (or cuts) which accumulate to create a huge amount of stress that is simply unbearable. Small stressors may actually be more dangerous than big ones since they are not as prominent—you may not even notice them until it is too late! It is important to recognize and take action to circumvent these stressors in your life. Let's start by simply breathing.

The Power of Oxygen

Oxygen is the key to life. Without it, we could not survive. But we are rarely aware of how we are breathing and what effect it has on our overall health. We all deal with some level of stress (which I liken to *chemical warfare*), especially in the workplace, but practicing self-care can be as simple as taking one deep, full breath.

According to Wikipedia, humans breathe approximately 23,000 times per-day. So if you are able to improve just one thing, improving your breathing could have a huge impact on your life.

Many people (including myself), have a shallow breath. This poor airflow restricts the body from getting the oxygen that it needs. As a result, your blood and fluids do not reach all parts of your body, causing blocks and inflammation in the body. If this low-grade inflammation is in the body for long periods of time, it can create illness and disease. Oxygen is the key to prevent this!

> *"All chronic pain, suffering, and diseases are caused by a lack of oxygen at the cellular level."*
>
> —Dr. Arthur C. Guyton

The breath has the ability to transform your chemical and energetic state immediately into a state of relaxation. In a Forbes.com article, Towers Watson said, "Breathing is a great way to manage stress. Experts recommend taking deep breaths for a few minutes to help lower your current stress level. I mean, you're already breathing anyway so why not make use of all of the benefits!"

Notice the quality of your breath when you feel anxious or stressed at work. Perhaps your boss has been on your case about a deadline, or a coworker is gossiping, and you are trapped listening to their negativity. Is your breath high up in your chest, shallow, and fast? This is actually a state of fight or flight, an ancient response that the reptilian part of your brain uses to keep you safe from predators. But there aren't any tigers chasing you at work in this day and age, right? This response is not needed anymore!

The WealthFlow Code is all about taking radical responsibility for your well-being. It's up to you to calm down your nervous system because only you can track how you feel and the state of your breathing. So the next time you notice yourself in a fight or flight response with shallow, high breathing, stop and feel your feet on the floor. Get grounded. Try breathing slowly and more deeply into your belly instead of high up in your chest. This way of breathing is how the body moves energy. Make a conscious choice to use deep breathing to expand into a more free, easy and flowing state rather than contracting and shutting down into constriction and tightness. By adding more oxygen into your blood, you will feel calmer, more energized, and lighter.

"Employees who have high stress levels at work also have lower engagement, are less productive, and have higher absentee levels than those not operating under excessive pressure."

—Isaac M. O'Bannon, author of *3 Ways High Stress in the Workplace Leads to Lower Productivity**

*see *Resources* on page 111

3 Steps to Reduce Stress

1. Stop and feel your feet on the floor.

2. Get grounded.

3. Breathe slowly and deeply into your belly instead of high up in your chest.

If your company offers meditation or yoga classes, this can be a helpful way of cultivating a deeper, more nourishing way of breathing. If not, then you can always find a local yoga studio or meditation group to join. There are also many online resources (see *Resources* on page 111). Be proactive and find community to support you as you make these lifestyle changes and build new habits.

"When the breath is unsteady, all is unsteady; when the breath is still, all is still. Control the breath carefully. Inhalation gives strength and a controlled body; retention gives steadiness of mind and longevity; exhalation purifies body and spirit."

—Goraksasathakam

Know Your Numbers

When I realized that you can use tools to test your body and see how much oxygen it is receiving, I rushed out to purchase a finger pulse oximeter which I use to measure my oxygen levels during tax season. So when I feel really stressed, I can simply put the tool on the end of my finger and see how my body is being affected by stress. This confirms for me when I need to take a meditation break, a walk, or simply do some slow, deep breaths. After doing this, I found a book called *Reboot Your Health* by Sara Davenport, where she reveals an oxygen tester tool along with several other do-it-yourself (DIY) tests and solutions to assess and improve your health. Davenport suggests to "get an accurate reading by checking four times a day over five days. Aim for a 94-99 percent level." By knowing your normal rate, you will know when your body is out of balance.

Look for the Signs: The Sea of Awareness

Since I have learned to follow my internal guidance, I receive many daily signs from the universe. Sometimes I will see an actual sign on the side of the road, or a license plate, an email message, an animal, or a repeating number like 555 or 222. These signs help me to connect to my center and trust my intuition.

At one point, I received the same ad via email for oxygen tanks used by the elderly over and over again. It took me a few days to realize that this was a message from the universe to deepen my breath and receive even more oxygen. Once I became aware of it, the ads stopped!

"Breathing affects your respiratory, cardiovascular, neurological, gastrointestinal, muscular, and psychic systems, and also has a general effect on your sleep, memory, ability to concentrate, and your energy levels."

—Donna Farhi

Now that I am less stressed, more present, and more focused on listening to my body and breathing deeply, it's much easier to get things done in less time. Proper breathing has helped me to go from an exhausted mess to an energized powerhouse! Gain mastery over the breath and you will gain control of your life force energy.

Create More Efficiency

I have found that during stressful times at work, especially while working long hours during tax season, connecting to my center helps me be more efficient.

When I am able to get into this *flow* state, I can get more done with less effort. *Flow* is about balancing your energy so that you are not just using your left-brained, masculine energy to push through projects, but instead also accessing your right-brained feminine energy and relaxing into your creativity. This balance of masculine and feminine energies allows you to sail through stressful times with much more ease and grace. This is referred to as the Universal Law of Gender—yin and yang—and is based on the Chinese philosophy of Taoism.

It took me more than 50 years to discover the Tao!

I grew up in a yang-dominated environment, where everything was about pushing through to get things done... definitely more of the male energy. I always wanted to be more like my sister who I believed had more feminine qualities than me. But my father wanted a boy, so I may have subconsciously been trying to please him by being more yang. This yang energy dominated me growing up, in my former marriage, with my two sons, and in my career as an accountant.

As I've witnessed my nieces over the years, I can see how they differ in their way of thinking and in their creativity. I now understand that this is divine feminine, or *yin* energy. In recent years, I have been incorporating more yin (feminine) energy into my life to be more balanced in giving and receiving. Having a network and supportive community of women around me has helped me cultivate more yin in my being. I help other women whenever possible so I can be of service, and they reciprocate in these giving (yang) and receiving (yin) relationships.

Recently I bought roses for myself and felt compelled to give a rose to one of my female associates who was having a difficult day. She accepted the rose and thanked me over and over! I was surprised, as I didn't see how it was that big of a deal. But to her, that small gesture activated happiness and gratitude.

The act of giving is just as gratifying, if not more so, than receiving...

The State of Gratitude

"When you realize there is nothing lacking,
the whole world belongs to you."

—Lao Tzu

Practicing gratitude for what we already have in our lives attracts more of the good things to us. Daily gratitude is a time-tested practice to help you master the art of giving thanks every day. By cultivating the power of deep appreciation, gratitude becomes a simple and natural way of life for you. In addition, you can also be grateful for things you don't have yet but want to attract into your life. I practice gratitude daily in my morning meditation ritual and before bed to set myself up for excellent sleep. I will share more about *how* I do this in the tools below.

Thinking positively is the first step to finding inner peace and sets you up to receive what you are grateful for. It's about giving thanks for what you already have and manifesting something else into your life *before it actually exists*. Try to dwell in gratitude for everything that happens to you, both the good *and* the bad.

Here are two exercises to try when you wake up in the morning and before you go to bed at night:

1. **Write down three things you are grateful for or start a group text with friends or family** and do this together each day. I text my two sons what I am grateful for and they text me and share what they are grateful for. This is a perfect way for *all* of us to focus on the positive, and that is exactly the vibration of what we attract back to us. Know that there is something to learn in each experience you have, so you can uncover those lessons with more grace and less pain by simply having this awareness and being grateful for the lesson you receive. The more you focus on everything you are grateful for, the less room there will be in your life for worry and stress. This concept is related

to the law of attraction. Whatever you focus on expands because *like attracts like.* So be sure to focus on the positive (or the lesson) and not on the negative.

2. **Do a visualization exercise every morning before you get out of bed.** Simply visualize what you want to happen in your day and how you want it to unfold. Be intentional with your thoughts—this can be quite powerful! During your visualization, activate all five senses so you can really feel like you are there and it is actually happening. Set an intention and then visualize it as if it has already happened. Choose a date you want it to happen by and feel the feelings you will have when it is here (i.e. excitement!)

"Gratitude in advance is the most powerful creative force in the Universe."
—Neale Donald Walsh

"It is believed in the science of Echo Psychology that a rise in depression and other mental spiritual illnesses in this day and age is due to the increase in technology and development, keeping people disconnected from the earth... When our Earth Element within is sick, we are unable to receive nourishment both mentally and physically from the world around us. When the Earth is out of balance our ability to nourish and take care of ourselves and others is impaired. For example, we can expend too much energy taking care of others and leave nothing for ourselves."

—Worsley, J.R., author of *The Five Elements and the Officials*

The Universal Law of Gender

Universal laws govern the movement of energy. The Universal Law of Gender shows us that all things, regardless of gender, have both masculine and feminine energies (yin and yang). To create, we need a balance of both masculine and feminine energy. This law tells us that everything in nature is both male and female. All things require space, time, and nurturing to grow. For example, when we plant a seed (masculine) it requires time to grow and manifest (feminine). This is the law that requires patience and persistence and tells us not to give up before the goal is reached. Instead of pushing through to get something done (masculine energy), we can incorporate some feminine energy as well, (like creativity or even resting) to make it easier to accomplish our goals. *When these two forces are in alignment, the power is amplified.* In *Sacred Powers—The Five Secrets to Awakening Transformation,* author Davidji describes this as "A pathway out of your challenges and into a space of freedom, happiness, and lasting fulfillment."

You can activate your awareness, focused attention, set intentions, and then take action toward the intention. In this way, you are making progress to transform your life.

"Attention is the activator of intention, intention is the spark of transformation, and action converts the energy flow into your tangible reality."

—Davidji, author of *Sacred Powers: The Five Secrets to Awakening Transformation**

**see *Resources* on page 111

Take one small step each day toward your goal for three days until it becomes a habit. This is how we can bring our goals and dreams into our physical reality. You may have heard the saying "As above, so below"... that's what we are doing here. It's like pulling the dream through to the physical 3D realm to be manifested into reality.

Integration of Yin and Yang

When I went on a relaxing vacation for a few weeks, I came back and went right back to work midweek. I was living from a yin perspective while on vacation (meditating, practicing yoga, and listening to my intuition). When I got home, I started to declutter my closets. I later learned that this is a form of integrating from vacation (yin) back into work (yang). I realized, however, that I could have scheduled in an extra day or two to *reintegrate* into my work environment—which is very yang—because *clearly,* the amount of time I had (less than one day) wasn't enough!

After my first day back at the office, I had to readjust myself in order to balance out the yin and yang in my system. Those two days back to work (before the weekend *finally* arrived) left me stressed out, overwhelmed and exhausted! So I used several of my tools over the weekend and also booked a massage to realign myself and my chakras to get back into balance. Here are some tools for you to connect to your center:

1. **Circle of Life Assessment**—This exercise will give you a clear visual picture of where your life is thriving, and what areas could use a little more attention. How it works: Using the circle provided, place a dot within each section to mark how satisfied you are with that area of your life. A dot placed towards the center of the circle indicates dissatisfaction, while a dot placed towards the outside indicates happiness. Once you've placed a dot within each section, connect the dots and see your Circle of Life. Please place a dot in all areas, all are required (see *Resources* on page 111).

2. **Walk in Nature**—Walking in nature is a wonderful way to connect to your center. I have found that when I walk outside in nature, I can get into the FLOW state more quickly each time. Because I have walked so much at work over the last few years, my body knows the routine and *expects bliss.* And so as soon as I step outside and begin to walk, my body calms down and I begin to breathe much deeper than I otherwise would have if I stayed in the office. This is so healthy and rejuvenating! And when I return to my desk, I have a fresh new perspective and sense of balance between my body and my mind that gives me clarity around my work. It is a state of presence. My energy declines at about 3pm daily so that is when I go for a walk. When I return from my walk, I usually have

a cup of green tea with a little honey. 3pm is also a perfect time because it balances out a long day—especially when I have to work into the evening during tax season.

3. **Breathing Exercise**—Most of the time, we are not aware of our breath. Practicing a breathing exercise and paying attention to the breath is something I found extremely helpful while walking. However, you can do this at any time of day practically anywhere. Simply stop and take three deep breaths in through your nose and expand your belly, then blow the air out through your mouth on the exhale. You can visualize breathing in peace and breathing out stress. It is a way to be present in the moment, not worrying about the past or the future. I often refer to this as "NOW" time.

4. **Breathe and Connect Grounding Exercise** (Root Chakra)—Go into nature whenever possible. With your feet flat on the ground and sitting up with your back straight (vertical to the ground), breathe in through your nose and expand your belly out, hold your breath at the top for a few seconds and then breathe out through your mouth and push all of the air out of your body and bring your belly button flat to your spine. Connect to the earth envisioning roots growing out from your feet down into the earth and wrapping around the planet. Then visualize white light coming down from the sky and into the top of your head. See the white light flowing down through your crown to your third eye, past your throat, your heart and down into your solar plexus until it reaches your sacral chakra and finally your root chakra. Imagine that the roots coming up from your feet are connecting with the white light coming down through your head at your heart space. Feel the love and compassion and oneness of everything in the Universe. You are connected above and below like a bridge. *This is how you can get out of your head and drop into your heart. As above, so below.*

Do these exercises often in order to stay in the *flow*. You'll experience greater productivity and ease in getting things done without fighting against the tide. Instead, the tide is flowing, and you are riding the waves with it. Imagine that you are one with the Sea, consciously aware and in perfect alignment and harmony. This practice will also help to cultivate inner peace, trust, and faith in your everyday life.

Meditations

Meditation allows you to ground your energy so that you can align your chakras and get your foundation (root chakra) in balance. Your root chakra is at the base of your spine and is often referred to as the color red. It represents safety and security in the world. By doing these simple meditations, you will ground and rejuvenate, and fill up your energy so that you can serve from a full cup. Remember that if your energy is depleted, you cannot help others. Read through the following meditations first, and then I would suggest recording all of the following meditations on your phone so that you can meditate with more focus and presence. Or, simply visit **www.juliannejoy.me/wealthflowcodegifts** for the downloadable audio recordings and load onto your phone.

A morning meditation practice is a great way to start the day off right. Quieting your mind and trying to find the gap between your thoughts is quite challenging, but it can be simple. I find it to be like doing yoga.

Morning Light Meditation

Access free recording online at:
www.juliannejoy.me/wealthflowcodegifts

I invite you to find a comfortable seated position, with your feet flat on the ground. Close your eyes and focus on your breath. Just notice on your inhale how your body expands and how on the exhale you release. Inhale again, holding your breath at the top, and exhale release. Inhale again and expand your belly as you breathe in, hold it at the top of your breath, exhaling as you bring your belly button to your spine. And as you do this, just focus on your breath. Just like that. Every breath, every sound, every word takes you deeper and deeper and relaxes you more and more. It feels so good to be safe and relaxed. Now, I'd like you to imagine yourself sitting on a beach. It's a perfect day, with the warm sun shining on your face and you can hear the sound of the waves in the background crashing on the shore. You can see white seagulls flying above you in the crystal-clear blue sky as you breathe in the refreshing ocean air. You are so relaxed and at peace. Then you decide to climb some nearby rocks and notice that you are on the top of a cliff and you have a view where you can see in all directions. There is nothing that you cannot see. And from this perspective, you realize that there aren't any problems that you cannot solve. As you walk back to the ocean, you climb onto your raft where you begin floating and drifting with the tide. It feels so good to be held and supported by the water and mother earth. You are feeling so nurtured and comfortable that you fall asleep, and when you wake up, you're surrounded by beautiful palm trees and the sound of a waterfall. You realize that you have floated to one of the most beautiful places in the world! There are fruit trees all around you. So you gently pull down the fruit from a tree and bite into it. The sweet nectar spills out filling your mouth and lighting up your taste buds. As the sun is setting, you see the beautiful orange, pink, and purple colors. Open your eyes slowly and just notice how you feel.

Root Chakra Meditation

Access free recording online at:
www.juliannejoy.me/wealthflowcodegifts

Close your eyes and receive the breath into your body. Notice your chest relaxing and your face relaxing. Take another inhalation and direct that life force all the way down to your root chakra. Keep your focus there and inhale again, and direct that energy again into your root chakra. See roots growing from your feet and wrapping around the earth. Notice the quality of those roots... are they thick, thin, curly? On the next inhale, through those roots, bring in grounding earth energy up to your root chakra, the one that keeps you grounded and safe. See a red energy building up in your root chakra. Notice how wonderful it feels to be completely grounded. On the next inhalation, bring in earth energy into your sacral chakra. Begin to see an orange light. Notice if there are any areas of darkness or shadow and just with your intention, smooth those out so they are completely open. Notice that part of your body, just below your belly button, being filled with this delicious orange light. Take another deep breath and bring it up into your solar plexus. Begin to see or feel a yellow light. Again, notice if there are any shadows. If you do, breathe in a stronger golden yellow light to balance out any shadows and see your chakra completely balanced and feel this luminous personal power at your solar plexus chakra. Take another breath into your first chakra, second chakra, solar plexus, and all the way up to your heart. Begin to see and feel that green light at your heart chakra. Begin to notice if there is any darkness or shadow and begin to expand in your chest and open up your heart to give and receive unconditional love. On the next inhalation bring your attention up to your throat and begin to see a turquoise light. With just your intention and your breath, make that light stronger, opening up your throat, your neck, so you can speak your truth, ask for what you want, express and live your purpose. Feel that tingling sensation in your throat as new messages come to you in little whispers. On the next inhale, begin to see a blue light opening right between your physical eyes, so that you can see beyond the physical world. So that you can see what you need to see. On the next inhale, bring all your attention to your crown and see or feel a purple light. Again with your intention, make that purple light really strong, completely open, and connected. Take a look at all your chakras completely balanced, staggered all one on top of the other, vibrating exactly the way they need to be. On the next inhale, you will bring earth energy again through your roots and up through all of your chakras until you reach your crown. As you reach the crown, feel an opening above your head, and as the energy passes through that opening it becomes white light that goes into the universe. And on the next inhale, you draw that white light from the universe back into your crown and down through all of your chakras. Just notice how your whole body is vibrating and pulsating as this energy is going into every cell of your body. This white light has the capacity to change any aspect of your life. It has the magnitude to allow you to manifest and bring forth your dreams in alignment with your purpose and your highest power, as you're feeling that energy move through your entire body, feel and know that you are completely aligned. Slowly open your eyes and notice how you are feeling. Namaste.

Grounding Meditation

Access free recording online at:
www.juliannejoy.me/wealthflowcodegifts

Take a deep belly breath breathing in through your nose and out through your mouth. Visualize that you are connected to the planet like a tent with guide-wires coming out from each arm and extending to and around the earth...and you are breathing in a white light of peace through your nose, and breathing out love through your mouth and into the world. Surround yourself in a bubble of white light and visualize your energy and vibration being raised. See this white light coming in through your feet from the earth, up your spine and out the top of your head. On your next breath, imagine there is an opening at the crown of your head, and that yellow sunshine is entering the top of your head and filling every part of your body. This energy is a warm, glowing yellow energy, healing every cell of your body. Feel it in your head, your throat, your arms, your heart, solar plexus, sacral chakra, root chakra and all the way down into the earth. Open your eyes slowly and you should feel more aligned, relaxed, and balanced.

Syncing up with the Rhythms of the Earth, Sun and Moon

The entire universe is made of energy. Ancient Chinese medicine emphasizes the importance of timing our behavior, both hourly and seasonally, according to the cycles of the earth, sun, and moon.

We can support the changes in the body caused by our life force energy (Qi) and blood flowing to different organs and meridians at specific times of the day by doing what is good for the body during that time period and avoiding things that might harm the body.

Even though the body appears to be a material object, in reality it is a field of energy. We must manage our own energy levels so that we have reserves. It is important to recognize where we are energetically. By combining ancient wisdom with modern science and following the circadian rhythms—

your body's internal clock—you will be able to identify the time of day that your energy is high or low.

When you follow your body's natural cues to go to sleep and wake up, you will stay in balance. It helps to stick to a consistent sleep schedule and waking up at the same time every day. You can go for a morning walk to get an energy boost from the sun. Try limiting evening technology since bright lights can throw off your body clock, or try blue light reading glasses.

The **Meridian Health Clock App** (see *Resources* on page 111) indicates each meridian in your body by hour of the day and suggests what you should and should not do during those hours. You can notice what time of day you are most focused and productive and then use that time to work on the most difficult projects. Learn to say "no" to diversions and trivial addictions like watching TV or surfing on your phone. This app also offers suggestions for the times of day that are best to eat and when to stop eating.

Another helpful tip is to break large projects down into smaller pieces and schedule them onto a timeline.

"As we age, our circadian clocks weaken. This age-dependent deterioration of circadian clock parallels our increased risk for metabolic diseases, heart diseases, cancer, and dementia. But the good news, says the researchers, is that a simple lifestyle change such as eating all food within 10 hours can restore balance, stave off metabolic diseases, and maintain health."

—www.ScienceDaily.com

The book, *Change Your Schedule, Change Your Life* by Dr. Suhas Kshirsagar is a fabulous resource for this!

Energy Reboot

Claim your power by bringing more life force energy into your being. If you can sustain high levels of energy, you can attract better circumstances and have more power to practice self-care, serve others and have more self-confidence. Most people look at life as a linear timeline where you are born at one end of the timeline and die at the other end. Another perspective would be to look at life as a circular timeline, like a circle or an infinity symbol. You use energy and then fill yourself back up, which is a circular pattern that allows you to live longer and age more gracefully—and perhaps even reverse the aging process! One of my clients recently had a birthday, and when I shared this perspective on life as a circular pattern with her, she was eternally grateful and asked if she could share it with others because it resonated with her so deeply. I personally have felt that I am getting younger ever since I began the exercises in this book. I most definitely feel very young at heart and I wish that for you, too!

Recharging Your Batteries

Think of your chakras as invisible, rechargeable batteries. By practicing an energy exercise you can recharge your battery and fill yourself up. Some of the tools I have used are Qigong, Reiki, and an energy medicine routine by Donna Eden. These are simple practices that you can learn and incorporate into your life. I found that doing them in the morning was helpful for me and a great way to start every day. So I suggest that you create a morning routine (or ritual) to support yourself.

I have been playing with my morning routine for years now, and as time goes on, I modify the routine based on new modalities that I learn such as kundalini yoga or various energy medicine practices. Walking on the treadmill or in nature keeps me balanced and in shape. I also lift weights and do yoga. Yoga connects your mind with your body which is truly invigorating! When you listen to your body, it will tell you what it needs. When you try different things, you can *feel* into them to see what makes your body sing. Then you know it is something you should continue doing. You may want to change your routine periodically since your body is constantly changing and may need different practices at different times of the year. *Have fun and play with it!* My newest joy is dancing, which puts me in a high vibration. I danced in the morning and before bed each night during tax season to increase my energy levels, maintain a high vibration, and release any stress from the day for a good night's sleep.

Gratitude Practice

Gratitude comes in many forms and can be practiced at any time of the day. However, I find that doing it in the morning sets up my day for success and doing it again before bedtime sets me up for sleep success. Start by writing down three things that you are grateful for in your gratitude journal in the morning and again at night before bed. They should be different items each time—and can be absolutely anything!

I recently purchased a mala bead bracelet at the hotel spa while traveling. There are eighteen beads on the bracelet. During my morning meditation, I began using the bracelet to help me count when repeating the phrase "Thank You" 108 times and kept track by touching each bead and repeating this exercise with the bracelet six times. The next day I changed the mantra to "I AM Calm, Relaxed, and Balanced". You can replace the mantras above with any phrase that resonates with you in the moment. This practice is helping me *live from the inside out* and to be grateful for everything in my life—it can help you, too! There are so many ways to practice gratitude. Here are some simple ideas to help you:

1. Keep a gratitude journal.

2. Thank someone for helping you by sending them a text, email, giving them a call, or sending them a *handwritten* thank you note.

3. Be thankful for your pet who offers you unconditional love—*through thick and thin.* Give them some extra attention and love.

4. Pause before meals to be grateful for the food you are about to eat, as well as everyone who prepared it.

5. Do a good deed or pay it forward (i.e. hold the door or pay for the next person in line at the coffee shop).

6. Run your errands with gratitude and let everyone know how grateful you are for their help (cashiers, bank tellers, grocery baggers, etc.).

7. Take a walk in nature and practice gratitude for your surroundings (i.e. the fresh air, the warm sun, or the luscious foliage).

8. Use each bead of a mala bead bracelet or necklace as a counter as you repeat your intention or mantra 108 times.

Creating Sacred Space

By creating an area in your home or office where you can connect with yourself, decompress through meditation, or practice your morning routine, you will become more effective and clearer on your path. Having a place where you can go to connect with yourself and the earth is as crucial as any other room in your home. It could be an altar or just a meditation pillow in a peaceful area of your home, or a spot outside that feels tranquil to you. When you go to the same place to meditate, or do whatever healing work that speaks to you, there is an energy that builds up over time. It triggers your mind to feel soothed the moment you enter the space because it subconsciously recognizes it as a space for relaxation. Whatever objects you place in your space will hold that energy for you.

When setting up your sacred space, it is best to incorporate things that will connect you to your senses. For sight and touch, you can bring in objects that you love. For smell, bring in a diffuser with essential oils or use candles. For sound, play a tranquil CD or high frequency music such as theta healing music. I like to make my own music playlists, and I suggest you do the same!

We must be the change we want to see in the world by being reflective and proactive versus reactive. Once we stop rushing through life, we will be amazed how much more life we have time for. Inhale, then exhale. That's how you'll get through it. And always remember to breathe deeply!

Root Chakra (1st)

- I am Safe
- Survival
- Color: red

Your root chakra is located at the base of your spine. When this chakra is open, we feel rooted, safe, secure, and fearless. It is represented by the color red and the sense of smell (*Hint: I noticed that I can become very grounded when I inhale my essential oils during meditation practice.)* The root chakra is an earth element—one of the four elements of earth, fire, water, and air). The root chakra represents the "grounding" of your being in the material world. It's your strong foundation and it represents your will to survive (fight or flight), self-preservation, presence, and prosperity. When you are rooted, then your life can really blossom, just as a red rose will be able to unfurl her petals and blossom, due to her strong stem and nourished roots.

We need to be playful and joyful to keep the root chakra open.

When we are in a state of joy, we attract abundance back to us just like a magnet. Think of yourself as an antenna. Whatever vibration you put out is the vibration you attract back to you. *You are creating your own life.*

Root Chakra Tools

*see *Resources* on page 111

- Walking in nature (barefoot is best)
- Swimming in the saltwater at the beach
- Creativity (such as drawing, art or dancing for example)
- Yoga poses: warrior pose, tree pose*
- Essential oils: Cedarwood, Cypress, Balance, Vetiver, Frankincense*
- Daily Root Chakra Meditation*
- Grounding Meditation*

Journal Entry – October 31, 2017

Organize your tools and everything in your environment so you have what you need, when you need it, to create a feeling of support in your life.

Ask for Support—Notify and Educate Your Network

"Ask for help not because you're weak, but because you want to remain strong."

—Les Brown

Your Personal Support System

Creating a personal support system will help you to help others. On an airplane, we are instructed to put our oxygen mask on first before helping anyone else. This is important advice because if we don't do this, we can become depleted and may not have the energy or strength to give to others.

Unplug Yourself

During busy, stressful times in your life, you can plan to unplug ahead of time and ask for support from your friends and family. You can also let others know that you may be off email and social media for a period of time. Educate your network about your schedule and how they can help support you, the best times to contact you, and times that are off limits (i.e.

around tax deadlines). During tax season, I unplug from social media and electronics to reduce stimulation to my sense organs and to give my mind a needed rest.

Educate Your Network

It is important to let your family, friends, coworkers, and clients know *in advance* about your schedule and needs. This way, they can help to support you. By notifying and educating your network, you are creating a personal support system. During this time, you may also want to limit other activities in order to rest and recover. However, do not limit the things that fill you back up, like your morning routine, exercise, meditation, massages, creativity, and cultivating time for rest and play or any other practices on your list that put you in the *flow*.

Follow your bliss and fill up with whatever creates a state of joy in you. These types of practices will create more time freedom for you because when you go with the flow rather than pushing against it, you can get more done in less time.

Collaboration and Teamwork

Surround yourself with positive relationships. By cultivating a collaborative team, you can work together cohesively so that it will take less time and effort to get things done, just as the birds that fly in V-formation conserve energy during their long, difficult journeys.

Researchers have determined that pelicans that fly in group formation beat their wings less often and have lower heart rates than those that fly alone. In her article "Why do Bird Flocks Move in Unison?" on **livescience.com,** Remy Melina shares that the same is true for humans! People who work together and support each other can often get more done with less effort than those working on their own. Celebrate your differences in relationships and teams since one person's weakness may be another person's strength.

Capitalize on the strengths of everyone on your team!

During tax season or times when we are working on larger projects, it is so important to have collaboration and teamwork in order to get the work done more efficiently. We can break large projects down through simplification into more manageable tasks and create a timeline with attainable due dates. This way, we can see more progress along the way with milestones instead of waiting until getting to the end of a project.

With open communication, delegation, and by capitalizing on people's strengths, we can get more done with less time and effort. It is important that each team member take on their role, as each person represents a cog in the wheel. When one of the team members doesn't pull their weight, it can be extremely counterproductive to the others on the team. It can feel like a boulder on your back having to do other people's work! And, it can put you into overwhelm, powerlessness, and disrupts the container of people who are relying on each other. Teamwork is so important! Finding the balance between self-care and your duty/connection to coworkers requires communication and a culture of collaborative teamwork.

Structuring Your Calendar—Systems Engineering

When there is a lot to get done, focus on having more structure in your routine, and avoid procrastination. It often takes more time to get tasks done when procrastination derails you from starting the task. One of my favorite time management strategies is called the Pomodoro Technique. It involves setting a timer for 25 minutes to stay focused on a task during that time and then taking a 5-minute break. I recently began using the **Focus Keeper App** (see *Resources* on page 111) to assist with writing this book. *The timer gave me a goal to beat, which helped me break through procrastination!*

"Procrastination is the thief of time."

—Edward Young

Structure and planning are important and necessary so that you do not get out of balance and caught up in overwhelm. By adding these organization tools, you can create systems to help you through difficult periods in your life and accomplish more with less effort and time. You can do tasks in batches or time chunks. When something unexpected comes up, be sure to ask yourself this question: *Does this need to be done now or can I schedule it into my calendar for the future?*

Streamline your schedule and improve communication with associates and family. Schedule in everything on your calendar, including your health appointments and self-care practices! If it's not scheduled, it's not real! So put yourself first by scheduling in your workouts and even your morning practice and daily meditation. Some examples of things I have incorporated are scheduling massages for the entire tax season in advance on my one day off (Sundays) ahead of time. Wearing daily contacts instead of monthly contacts helps my eyes with the long, straining hours of computer work needed to get through tax season. Exercising regularly on a daily basis gives me more energy and offsets the long periods of time that I am sitting at my desk. I have recently been using a stand-up desk which is also helpful because I am not sitting all day. Make an effort to get up and stretch at least once every hour.

Setting Boundaries and Learning to Say No

"A schedule defends from chaos and whim. It is a net for catching days...
A schedule is a mock-up of reason and order—willed, faked, and so
brought into being."

—Annie Dillard

Practice protecting your time, energy, and stress levels by setting boundaries. In *7 Habits of Highly Effective People*, author Stephen Covey shows us how to categorize tasks into four quadrants:

1. If it's important and urgent, always do it first.

2. If it's important but not urgent, do it soon.

3. If it's urgent but not important, delegate if possible, or do it if time allows.

4. If it is not important and not urgent, *never* do it.

Trim your to-do list by prioritizing your tasks with 3-5 must do's for each day. You must learn to say "no" because if you keep saying yes to requests, you'll end up with a never-ending to-do list with tasks that are not mission-critical for you or your team.

Be selective with meetings since they can kill your productivity. Ensure that each meeting has an agenda and specific needs to accomplish for the best use of your time. Delegate as much as possible to place less pressure on yourself. One bonus of this is that others will appreciate the faith you have placed in them.

Setting work-life boundaries is more productive than striving for work-life balance, according to Barrett Cordero, President of BigSpeak, Inc. He says "...the idea of balance presumes control over our environment—that our work and life demands come in predictable patterns. But work has deadlines and families have crises and sometimes more time is needed in one area of our life than the other."

This idea of work-life boundaries is about being 100% present at work and 100% present at home. It's important for management to lead by example and help set boundaries for their employees. Changing out of your work clothes as soon as you get home to physically transition from work to home is a great way to shift your energy.

Sometimes when we are around certain people, we may feel tired and drained afterwards, almost as if it's been stolen by vampires! If we can learn to set boundaries with these people, we can practice self-nurturance and assertiveness without being aggressive or defensive.

Organization: The Foundation of Your New Lifestyle

When we organize our outer physical world, it also has the positive effect of decluttering our inner mind. Time management can improve your quality of life. The key is to think ahead. Ask for and tap into the necessary skills you need so that you can effectively manage your life. Organizing yourself, family, home, work, and finances creates balance and inner peace.

I recently began to organize and declutter my home and office to prepare for the upcoming busy tax season. I broke it down into three steps:

1. Sort
2. Purge
3. Organize

First, I sorted all like items together. Then I purged anything that I didn't need or love. Marie Kondo's book *The Life-Changing Magic of Tidying Up* asks the question, "Does it spark joy?" Kondo's philosophy is that a person should only keep something if it sparks joy when you hold it. You can use three bins: 1) keep; 2) donate; or 3) throw away. Lastly, organize the keep pile for those things you use and love. Organize them in a way that provides easy access to them. The positive effect of having a clean, decluttered, and organized environment is very soothing to our minds and provides us with increased productivity.

Create Synergy with Your Sacred Space

It is important to create a space where you feel comfortable and at ease. We want our space to lift us, support us, and feel like our own personal haven. Your external space can have positive and healing effects on your health. Your space reflects your inner state. Use your creativity to create a sanctuary where you can relax, be inspired, feel a sense of flow, and thrive in your home or office environment. Our external world needs just as much attention and balancing as our internal world does, since they are a reflection of one another. There is synergy whereby when we change one, the other changes, too!

Many people are now using salt lamps in their offices. After speaking with a woman at a networking event recently, she told me that her husband wanted a salt lamp at his office in a manufacturing company because so many others were using them. The salt emits negative ions which bond with pollutants in the air and neutralize them. The negative ions also combat electro-smog caused by electronic devices and have a cleansing effect on your space by emitting calm lighting. These lamps also help heal and balance stress, migraines, tiredness, insomnia, and anxiety.

Try adding a diffuser with essential oils (see *Resources* on page 111), inspiring music, or use feng shui principles to remove clutter and add objects and colors to specific areas using the bagua map.

Creating sacredness in your space nourishes your soul, creates inspiration, vibrancy, and renewal.

Set up your physical environment with beauty and positive reminders that uplift your energy. Surround yourself with beauty all around you on the outside, in your physical environment, to have it reflect back to you on the inside, your internal environment. One simple action is to place fresh flowers in your workspace!

Sacral Chakra (2nd)

- I feel
- Creativity
- Color: orange

The second chakra, or sacral chakra, is located above the pubic bone but below the navel in the lower abdomen. It relates to the sense of taste and is the color orange. The sacral chakra represents the kidneys, which cleanse the blood and are vital for a healthy immune system.

This chakra also represents the power of relationships, emotional stability, flexibility, creativity, and the way we interact with others on a social level. The sacral chakra is about self-worth and is responsible for our creative expression. The element related to this chakra is water, representing co-hesiveness in relationships. When your root chakra is balanced, then your sacral chakra will have an easier time staying in balance. When the sacral chakra is out of balance, you may experience emotional instability, fear of change, depression, or addictive tendencies. You will not be able to connect to your higher self if these two lower chakras are not functioning properly. It is impossible to express your true nature, or essence, without this chakra fully open and uninhibited.

One way to open this chakra is through creative expression. Try playing and creating as if you were a child again!

Sacral Chakra Tools

- Notify your network about how busy you will be and ask for their support during this time.
- Schedule appointments for massage and other bodywork to take care of yourself during your busy time.
- Drink more water.
- Celebrate the milestones you've reached!

The Universal Law of Cause and Effect

Every action has a reaction. Every cause has its effect and every effect has its cause. Everything happens according to this law. Any action produces or returns a result or outcome in exact proportion to the act or cause which initiated it. So by taking action and asking for support, we receive a reaction or response to our request which sets us up for success. By practicing extreme self-care, we are demonstrating our value and self-worth, so that the universe can show us the positive effect of opening up the sacral chakra.

Create Divine Order in Your Space

Clear off your desk and clean out your inbox. The physical environment of your workspace has a significant effect on the way that you work. When your space is a mess, so are you. Libby Sander, author of "The Case for Finally Cleaning Your Desk" suggests that "...physical environments significantly influence our cognition, emotions, and behavior, affecting our decision-making and relationships with others. Cluttered spaces can have negative effects on our stress and anxiety levels, as well as our ability to focus, our eating choices, and even our sleep...with workplace stress costing American businesses up to $190 billion every year in health care costs alone, it's time to recognize the role that clutter plays in our work lives— and to do something to clean up the mess."

I know that when I have a clean, decluttered, and organized desk, it helps me to focus on one thing at a time and not worry about the other things that I need to do or multitask. Our brains like order, so constant visual reminders of disorganization can drain us and reduce our ability to focus. Clearing clutter from your work environment can help you focus and process information which will increase your productivity and reduce any procrastination. It can even stop avoidance strategies like mindless eating habits. Organized and decluttered desk equals an organized and focused mind! Once I cleared the clutter from my office and rearranged my furniture to make the room more spacious, I was so much more productive! My outer world was a reflection for my inner world.

Tips to Simplify, Declutter and Organize

- Set up an electronic library *blueprint* with files for easy access to information you may need later. Set up a flow chart to remember to use the library until it becomes a habit. Scan as much as possible so you can access it electronically from anywhere and have less paper clutter.
- Add candles and special lighting for focus and clarity.
- Add a diffuser with essential oils for aromatherapy benefits. I recently purchased a diffuser with a remote control, color-changing lights, and music!
- Add a Salt Lamp to diffuse the negative ions created from our devices (computers, cell phones, etc.).
- Use a stand-up desk—ideally for every 30-minute period, sit for 20 minutes, stand for 8 minutes, and walk for 2 minutes.
- Take a 5-minute yoga practice or chair yoga break.
- Yoga poses: pigeon pose, goddess pose*
- Essential oils: Ylang ylang, Orange, Clary sage, Ginger*

*see *Resources* on page 111

Structure Your Calendar

Plan ahead to make your calendar more effective. Identify when you're most focused and productive hours are (see "Meridian Clock App" in the *Resources* section) and do the most difficult projects during that time. Break down large projects into smaller blocks and add those blocks to your calendar. I recently began to color code my calendar which is making it more joyful. It is easier for me to glance at and know when my recurring appointments are since I use a color for each event. For example, I use pink for self-care and yellow for a weekly recurring meeting. So now I can identify with the colors as well as the words. This process makes it seem more like play and less like work! You can use a funnel calendar system where you list out all your tasks. Then you sort them by category and then prioritize them by assigning specific days for action by importance. You schedule them on your calendar to block out time to get things done.

Tools for Organizing

1. Schedule client meetings on the same day, resulting in less travel and interruptions on other days.

2. Work from home one day a week to gain focused quiet time since there is no need to commute and less interruptions.

3. Plan ahead and schedule meetings with staff on a weekly basis and as needed for client projects.

4. Plan time for *Rest and Recovery* (for me during tax season, this is Sunday).

5. Create structured time for *fun* and celebrations! Schedule a "Date Night" (for me this is Saturday nights).

6. Meal planning (make homemade soup once per week for healthy bone broth). Shop for the week and prepare meals in advance (see Step 5 on nutrition).

7. Eat with family a few nights per week and work from home after dinner. Work later at the office on opposite nights when meals are provided in order to be accessible to staff.

8. Delegate whenever possible and capitalize on your team member's strengths.

Journal Entry – Friday, July 8, 2016

I am claiming this weekend as a retreat for extreme self-care. While alone in my sacred space at the beach house in Rhode Island, I sat by the pool with a book for awhile, had a healthy and delicious dinner and watched a fabulous movie which brought up such a wide range of emotions for me that I both laughed and cried! I will get some exercise this weekend, read my books, get myself focused and organized with a plan, relax, and go to yoga and meditation on Sunday.

Listen to Your Body and Practice Extreme Self-care

"Self-care is not selfish. You cannot serve from an empty vessel."

—Eleanor Brown

The Power of Self-Care

Self-care is not an indulgence, it's a discipline. Your body knows what you need. It will give you subtle signs. But if you are not listening or taking any action, those signs may get more noticeable. It is very important to pay attention to these signs in order to avoid illness and depleted energy stores.

"Self-care requires tough-mindedness, a deep and personal understanding of your priorities, and a respect for yourself."

—Tami Forman

Self-care is not optional. Remember, if you don't take care of yourself, you cannot take care of anyone else. You must feel into your body, own it, and take action to care for yourself in order to be strong and resilient so you can be available to help and be of service to others.

Simple ways to begin to take better care of yourself is to get enough rest and exercise, eat healthy, and live mindfully. Tami Forman says, "It takes discipline to take full responsibility for your own well-being. Self-care can actually be kind of boring. It takes discipline to do the things that are good for us instead of what feels good in the moment. Some examples of self-care are saying "no" to the thing you don't want to do, even if someone is getting angry with you, declining the second drink at the office holiday party, maintaining financial independence, doing work that matters, and letting other people take care of themselves."

Self-care can also be a nuisance. We all know we should be drinking more water, exercising, getting enough sleep, eating healthier meals, and de-cluttering our desks! However, these things lack the urgency that looming deadlines and client phone calls bring. So you must be disciplined to do your self-care, which in fact, create the reserves from which you draw the stamina, creativity, mental clarity, and resilience we value (and get paid for) at work.

Living Mindfully

There are many ways to become mindful, such as meditating, practicing yoga (which creates the mind-body-spirit connection), exercising, or walking in nature. Mindfulness brings awareness to what is going on inside of you. Mindfulness helps us notice when we are judging others (or ourselves) or comparing ourselves to others. These are practices we need to release. Instead, we want to simply "observe" what is happening in a situation and "notice" why it is happening rather than judging ourselves for it.

"When we truly care for ourselves, it becomes possible to care far more profoundly for other people. The more alert and sensitive we are to our own needs, the more loving and generous we can be towards others."

—Eda Leshan

Perfectionism and the Power of Vulnerability

The perfectionism monster can be a nasty one! It can really hold us back from so many things in our lives. The WealthFlow Code shows another way: *Done* is better than *Perfect*! Sometimes, we don't even realize that procrastination is causing us to not write our book or be creative and paint because it hangs out in the subconscious waiting for a moment to strike!

I procrastinated on many creative projects in my life for years. I just felt stuck, never able to take action to move forward. Have you ever felt this way? Creativity requires vulnerability, which for me, has been a struggle. I have a room full of paints, art supplies, and creative projects which I have acquired over the years, but it was not until recently that I began to take action and use them again—*one small step at a time.* Even writing this book is about being creative and vulnerable! I never know exactly how my painting is going to come out, or even what I am going to paint. But when I am willing to be vulnerable and listen to myself, I *just do it!* I keep asking myself, *"What is the worst thing that can happen?"* The world will not end if we don't like the outcome of the painting or the book we've written! But if we never take action, we will miss out on sharing our wisdom and gifts with the world and being of service.

I am finally learning that perfectionism has been holding me back and when I am creative in all areas of my life, ideas flow to me much more easily. Once you start incorporating creative activities back into your life, you will notice a *huge* shift in your creative flow, inspiration, and motivation.

Being vulnerable is very difficult for me because I grew up being a perfectionist, Type-A personality with straight A's in school, making high honor roll and honor society, and always trying to please others. This is why I am so detail-oriented in my work and for years was only accessing the left brain (yang/masculine). Now that I understand how creativity works, I am adding in the right brain (yin/feminine) to create a cohesive dynamic duo to manifest more *joy* into my life.

Vulnerability requires a mindset shift and a willingness to tap into your creativity and openness. Being vulnerable can be scary but it is so worth it because creativity makes life more joyful and fun. Allow for more forgiveness, honor the process, and let it all be imperfect! Truthfully, there is no such thing as perfect. Perfection is an illusion and is self-sabotaging. Vulnerability allows me to switch out of my left brain and be in the *flow* state more often. It gets me out of my over-analytical mind and into my body to *feel!* But in order to feel, you must open your heart, and that doesn't always feel safe. So we have to take off our energetic shields of armor and be willing to be open and vulnerable.

In The Power of Vulnerability, author Brene Brown speaks to a "victim or viking mentality"—a mode of survival represented by daily fight or flight. Someone who has fought in a war is most likely living in a viking mentality, since they were taught that they are either a victim or a viking in the war. Unfortunately, many people live like this all the time, fighting to survive every day which releases an overabundance of cortisol, causing stress, inflammation, and disease in the body.

Finding Inner Peace through Creativity

Inner peace will not occur when our nervous systems are stuck in the "viking" mode of fight or flight. One way to find it is through heart-opening activities, such as those used in art therapy such as painting, photography, and other creative hands-on work. Studies show that PTSD in veterans is being treated successfully with art therapy. Creative activities such as art, dance, and writing are a few of the ways that I find inner peace, along with consistent meditation using essential oils, which have a direct connection to the soul through the olfactory senses—your sniffer! Using creativity to get in a *flow* state may be easier for you than meditation. Try different methods to see what works best for you.

We can also help others find peace simply by having our own peace first. Studying Taoism (a Chinese philosophy based on the writings of Lao-tzu advocating humility) has been very helpful for me. Taoism offers a single principle that underlies how everything happens—the "how". The method requires becoming aware of what is happening through meditation. *Silence* is a great source of strength. Can you learn to be open and receptive, quiet, and without desires or the need to *do* something? Being open and receptive is *yin* energy. Don't strive to figure things out with your mind. Instead, use intuition and reflection and stay in the present moment. When a person becomes calm and present, complex events appear simple. *See without staring.*

You Create Your Reality

In order to transform and create a new reality, something has to change, otherwise you'll stay in the same place, repeat the same old patterns, and continue to stagnate. You must change the paradigm (your system of beliefs, ideas, values and habits that affect the way you perceive the world) in order to create results. We are taught that our experiences lie on a linear timeline (past and future) and it is often difficult to stay present in each moment. But when you place your attention on the outside world, or the past or the future, your body will follow your mind to whatever you are thinking—to the known and comfortable, rather than the unknown and uncomfortable! For instance, when you focus on the past, it usually drains your energy like a siphon.

Our three-dimensional reality is made up of the known outer world (physical reality), whereas your *inner world* is full of your *thoughts and feelings.* If you put your attention on the *inner world,* you can create something new, rather than the same knowns. I am doing this through my daily yoga, meditation, and gratitude practice.

By staying present in the moment, you are not giving your power away to someone or something else in your life. Where do you place your energy and your attention on every day? We need to *disinvest our energy* in something *in order to change* it. This is why meditation is so powerful and can change your life.

How do you want to FEEL? Try playing with a desire map to identify what you want to attract into your life. Once you identify those feelings, then list out the activities and things that give you those feelings. For example, if you want more time, maybe you list out activities like work smarter, get organized, meditate and simplify. Be specific and break down each one into smaller steps and add them to your calendar to begin taking small daily action steps in the direction of your goals.

Change is Your Bridge

"The fastest way to still the mind is to move the body."

—Gabrielle Roth

Cultivating inner peace is about owning our own power. It's time to stop giving our power away to others and take back control of our own lives. We need to trust and have faith and know that change is actually good for us. If you can get into the flow of positive new experiences quickly, change will open the door and offer you a bridge to a new dream life.

One way to create change is through movement medicine, which **movementmedicineassociation.com** describes as "a body-based movement meditation practice that will reconnect you to the wisdom of living from the heart, the joy of knowing who you are and the satisfaction of making your unique contribution to life." With the freedom that you feel when you are dancing by connecting your mind with your body and your body with your heart, movement becomes medicine.

Gabrielle Roth's *5 rhythms* dance method is rooted in ancient wisdom and a modern understanding of how change happens. Its intention is to help you access more of the physical and emotional intelligence that's inside you, by bringing awareness to the way you move, feel and think. Movement can be your teacher, which lets you explore and feel more confident and free. The deepest challenge many of us have is to love ourselves for who we are. Dancing can create a massive amount of energy and help to melt your heart. You have a dancer inside of you that can connect you consciously to the whole spectrum of your being, take off the mask and connect you to the passion of your life. Whenever I had a block while writing this book, I listened to one of my favorite songs and danced. This helped to shift my energy and unblock my flow of sacred wisdom.

The Universal Law of Rhythm

Everything flows and vibrates in and out, rising and falling, backward and forward, action and reaction, high tide and low tide, advance and retreat, rising and sinking. This is rhythm. It's like a never-ending pendulum that swings to the left and to the right. These polarities and rhythms create our seasons. One can escape the effects of this Law to some degree by using it instead of being used by it. Emotional mastery is required for this. The Master attains a degree of poise or mental firmness by not getting too excited or allowing negativity into their consciousness, while the masses swing backwards and forwards like a pendulum. I like to think of the stock market flowing with this law of rhythm. There are times when it will go up and times when it will go down, but the key is to stay calm during the storm and not overreact and sell out—especially when you are in it for the long-haul.

Solar Plexus Chakra (3rd)

- "I Strive"
- Strength
- Color: yellow

The third chakra, or solar plexus chakra, is related to the sense of sight, metabolism, and the adrenal glands. It is the fire element, the color yellow, and is just below your heart and above your belly button. This chakra represents your emotions, self-esteem, trust, purpose, and your personal power. It regulates the use of food and helps the body adjust to stress.

When this chakra is blocked, you may lack confidence and worry about what others think. You may be depressed and will accept other people's negativity. However, when the solar plexus is spinning without obstruction, you will have a sense of personal power and it will bring respect and a cheerful and happy attitude that allows you to love challenges. So celebrate all of your successes, even the small ones. When we do this, we are sending out the energy to receive more success! Treat yourself as "First Class"—by doing this, you will teach others to treat you in the same way.

You can use your personal power and confidence to model for others how to follow their passion and live their purpose. Be humble, peel away the layers, and show the world who you really are with no fear of judgment...from anyone including yourself! Instead, be an observer. Notice if any judgment pops up in your mind, witness it, and then release it. Notice situations and be curious about them with a sense of wonder. When you are committed to attending to your state of awareness, everything falls into place.

When you peel away the layers of protection and instead tap into your vulnerability, you will experience the sweetest parts of life. Find out what is important to you. Create what you want! Feel the power of the Universe supporting you as you create adventures in your life. Find more joy and happiness than you ever thought possible, simply by aligning with what you value. Believe it and trust it! In order to trust, you must have faith. So always believe that something wonderful is about to happen. Believe it so you can receive it!

When you are passionate about life, others will be inspired by you. Live your legacy so others will live theirs!

Solar Plexus Chakra Tools

*see *Resources* on page 111

- Schedule periodic bodywork or massage to nourish your mind, body, and soul. Celebrate the milestones you've hit, such as getting through tax season!

- Yoga pose: boat pose.*

- Dance/movement meditation: Some examples are belly dance, Nia yoga (mind/body integration which combines dance and yoga), and 5Rhythms movement meditation developed by Gabrielle Roth.*

- Skating, surfing, or swimming...

- Get creative: draw, paint, color, write poetry, music, books...

- Essential oils: Lemon, Melaleuca, Peppermint, Rosemary, Ginger, Chamomile, Juniper. Try adding a few drops of the oil to the water in your diffuser and blissfully breathe in the fragrance.*

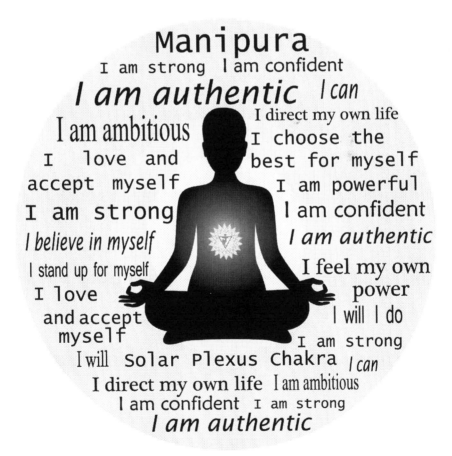

Journal Entry – November 11, 2017

The heart chakra is the power of love and emotion. Open your heart to live fully. Nurture yourself with extreme self-care, and others will treat you the same.

Accept Myself—
"I Connect to the Needs of My Body"

"Self-love is not selfish; you cannot truly love another until
you know how to love yourself."
—Anonymous

Connect to Your Body Wisdom

In order to cultivate an awareness around what your body is saying to you, listen to what it needs...but not from your head, from your *heart*. This requires getting still, contemplation, honing your intuition, and the willingness to honor your body's sacred heart wisdom. Follow the whispers.

Personally, I feel like I've had an ice fortress built up around my heart as a result of all of the challenges I have experienced in my life. And boy did I have to use *fire* to melt that ice in order to have an open heart, because that is where the magic is.

With the WealthFlow Code, I now have the ability to connect to my intuition and heart wisdom, instead of having to look for answers outside of myself—from someone else. Now I drop into my heart, listen, and feel. Your body will tell you the answer because your heart knows. It's time to trust yourself completely. Stop looking outside of you for answers and instead, look inward.

Practicing Extreme Self-Care

We receive signs and synchronicities from the universe all the time (divine intelligence in nature). If we choose to pay attention to them, we can interpret them and allow them to guide us along our path.

And...paying attention to the signs our bodies are giving us is *also* important. Listen to the signs and trust them. *Have enough self-love to do this!* Our bodies know what we need. But if we choose not to listen or pay attention, the outcome may not be good.

My body tells me when I need a break, especially at work. I get aches and pains in my back and sometimes I'll get an inner knowing that I need to go for a walk. I'll even stop what I'm doing, look outside to see if it's nice out, and then say to myself that I will go for a walk...as soon as I finish what I'm doing. But if I don't go when I first get the urge, the weather will usually turn and it will start raining or get dreary so that I can't go later, anyhow. The lesson? Listen to your intuition and inner knowing about what your body needs and do it NOW! Otherwise, you may miss out on receiving exactly what you needed in that moment.

I wasn't listening to my body when I had a bladder infection during tax season. I needed to get through a lot of tax returns and I was up against the wall without a minute to spare. I remember saying to myself, *"I will call the doctor as soon as I get done, right after tax season...I just need to get through this work to meet deadlines."* By waiting, I ended up at the walk-in emergency room and hospital on several occasions from that one event. I even had to go back because the medicine they had given to me didn't work.

Can you identify a time when you did not listen to what your body was telling you? When I didn't listen, I got sick. Now, I tune in, listen, and use my tools in order to get through unscathed. Here's the truth: You need to listen to your body in order to take care of it. Your body knows what it needs, and you must pay attention and take action without hesitation, rather than avoiding it. This is really about *self-love*. If you don't love yourself enough to take care of your body, you cannot take care of other people. You must take care of yourself first. As mentioned earlier in this book, we must always remember, just as flight attendants remind us in the airplane, "Put the oxygen mask on yourself first before helping the person next to you."

We really all just want safety and security—and we look to others to give it to us. But no one outside of us can really provide it, because freedom is an inside job! And it stems from your own sense of self-acceptance and self-love. When you truly embody self-love, the body will heal and your inner peace will be restored—this reflects your acceptance of love, rather than fear.

Preventing Burnout through Resilience

Resilience has been defined by the American Psychological Association as "The human ability to adapt in the face of tragedy, trauma, adversity, hardship, and ongoing significant life stressors." One key way to build resilience is to focus on self-care. *We can handle so much more and bounce back from challenges when we are taking care of ourselves.* Deep breathing, mindfulness, meditation, and yoga are all great ways to get through unexpected challenges. For example, if we can stay in the present moment by focusing on our breath instead of the issue while we process it, and then take a moment before we respond, this helps us to respond better. This allows us to use our body, as well as our mind, to feel into the issue and come up with a better solution. If we only use our mind, we are not using the power of our mind-body connection.

Overcoming adversity is not about *what happens to you*, but rather *how you respond* to it, so listening to our bodies and accepting ourselves without judgment is the precursor to personal freedom.

Tools for more resilience

- Make meaningful connections with family and friends.
- Exercise, follow a healthy diet, and use good sleep practices.
- Reframe how you view problems and obstacles (i.e. think of them as opportunities in disguise or challenges to learn and grow) and learn from these experiences.
- Give yourself a break from media—schedule *offline* time.
- Simplify your life with routines and organization and be proactive.
- Set boundaries and limits to protect your time and make time for simple pleasures like watching the sunset and playing with your pet.
- Practice relaxation techniques (meditation, mindfulness, deep breathing, yoga, etc.).
- Remain hopeful and positive.

Joy is My Compass: Practicing Self-Love to Strengthen Self-Worth

I realize that I have struggled with self-worth issues. This, combined with my need for perfectionism, is why, in my past, I was a workaholic and was not able to live with joy and happiness in my life. I was always worried about my next fight or challenge, wondering what would happen next that I would have to overcome... It was a pattern of negative thinking and focusing on thoughts that didn't serve me. But in fact I was actually attracting more of those negative situations into my life, just like a magnet.

Whatever you focus on expands. So once I realized that and started to focus on more positive thoughts and released my limiting beliefs, I was able to make the shift to attract better situations into my life and get out of that spiraling, never-ending pattern of things going wrong. I even started to buy myself flowers to show myself love and that I was worth it.

"If you follow your bliss, you put yourself on a kind of track that has been there all the while, waiting for you, and the life that you ought to be living is the one you are living. When you can see that, you begin to meet people who are in your field of bliss, and they open doors to you. I say, follow your bliss and don't be afraid, and doors will open where you didn't know they were going to be."

—Joseph Campbell

The Art of Balance

We can help others find balance simply by having our own balance first. Others will sense and see it in action as we model this behavior. By using *joy* as your compass for the next steps along your life path, you will honor yourself and honor others at the same time. It is a simple way to know which direction to go in. Simply ask yourself, "Does this give me joy?" If it does, that is a sign to move in that direction. There are no wrong steps because sometimes you need to take a step in a direction to find out that it is not the direction you want to take.

Build indestructible positivity by holding unconditional trust in everything that happens—understand that it is happening *"for you"* and not *"to you."*

Live in Joy! Joy is a state of BEING. When you are in a state of joy, you create abundance because you are attracting the same abundant joy to you.

"To strengthen the muscles of your heart, the best exercise is lifting someone else's spirit whenever you can."

—Dodinsky

Live with an Open Heart—Following Your Inner GPS

Follow your heart...it is your *inner GPS system*! Focus your mind (which is like a GPS) to get to your desired destination. You must have clarity without contradicting thoughts and beliefs. By stepping into your authentic self and living who you are truly meant to be (and not who others want you to be), you can live a more open-hearted life. You need to come out of hiding and stop living other people's lives. I used to hide behind other people, not stepping into my power or speaking up for fear of being judged. I had a sense of not being good enough and always looking outside myself for the answers rather than trusting myself and my intuition. In fact, it was really difficult for me to make any decisions on my own!

Once you start trusting yourself and listening to your intuition, you will be surprised to uncover all of the signs your body will give you to help you know the answers. Step into your power and speak your truth. Have trust and faith in yourself. Stop relying on everyone else. Feel how confident and powerful you are. Fear is simply something you need to get to the other side of. There are beautiful things waiting on the other side of fear. You can rise above it by using your imagination and visualizing this energy, which looks like a golden rose stream of light flowing up through your feet and into the center of your being, right up through your chakras. First, the root chakra, then the sacral and solar plexus, until it finally reaches your heart. Notice how it makes you feel so calm and relaxed with your heart expanding and opening to the beauty all around you. You begin to notice all of the abundance which was always there, but somehow not noticed. In fact, when we can intentionally surround ourselves with beauty on the outside, we will also have it inside of us because it lifts our vibration and puts us into a state of gratitude. When we appreciate, this puts us in a state of receiving more beauty and then sharing it with others. Be a vessel for Love!

Dancing and Trauma Release Exercise (TRE®)

During tax season while I was having a massage, my therapist was surprised that my body had become like a solid shield of armor. I couldn't even feel the massage! She told me to research TRE® (see *Resources* on page 111) and so I began to practice this trauma release exercise. I could feel the trauma most likely from past events in my life, bubbling up inside my body and this was a tool that I used to release it. I also danced most mornings and evenings (just before bed) to help me get through tax season. The dancing helped me to shift my energy to a higher vibration, release any old stagnant energy, and be in the present moment without worrying about the past or future. This helped me set up a successful day and sleep more soundly at night since I was able to remove all thoughts of worry and fear about the past and future from my mind just before my head hit the pillow each night.

Setting Boundaries

In order to live with an open heart, you must have boundaries. You need to trust when to say no and stop agreeing to do things that you *really* don't want to do. Stop tolerating rude comments or pushy people because you think that you cannot handle conflict. Don't take things personally. Life coach Cheryl Richardson shows you how to stand up for yourself, set personal boundaries, and free yourself from the "disease to please" with these three steps:

Step 1—Self-Awareness. "Pay attention to situations when you lose energy, feel a knot in your stomach, or want to cry. Identifying these situations is the first step."

Step 2—Setting Your Boundaries. You may need to find support before and after each conversation and should use specific language. "Start setting simple but firm boundaries with a neutral tone. It will feel uncomfortable at first, but as you take care of yourself, the personal power you gain will make it easier."

Step 3—Strengthen Your Internal Boundaries. Too often women neglect to stand up for themselves by avoiding confrontation. When someone offends you, stop and ask the following questions:

- How much of this is true about me?
- How much of this is about the other person?
- What do I need to do (if anything) to regain my personal power and stand up for myself?

By asking these questions, you will build your internal boundaries and have the ability to keep your power, rather than always giving it away to others.

The Universal Law of Polarity

Everything in life encompasses duality (polar opposites) like hot and cold, light and dark, love and hate, noise and quiet, high and low, negative and positive. These dualities are on the same continuum and include all the possibilities ranging from the negative to the positive spectrum. For example, you cannot experience sadness without knowing happiness, or hot without cold.

The law of polarity is a fundamental law of transformation and creation. It is important to know that we can transform negative thoughts through mental alchemy using the law of polarity by concentrating on the opposite (positive thoughts) pole. Christy Whitman says, "When you get rid of the bad to leave room for the good, applying the Law of Attraction, you are using the Law of Polarity to your own advantage, because the Universe hates a vacuum. When you get rid of something, you are making room for something else. What is emptied must also be filled."

Heart Chakra (4th)

- I am Loved
- Love
- Color: green

The heart chakra is in the center of your chest and represents love, empathy, and the seat of the soul. It is green in color and represents the thymus gland. It helps the immune system and its element is air. The heart is the organ that pumps blood and love through our entire body. It is the gateway to our higher consciousness, a bridge connecting body, mind, emotions, and spirit. The core of everything in the universe is love and is the ultimate truth. When the heart chakra is open, there is no such thing as fear or pain—only love, devotion, empathy, compassion, and friendship.

When the heart chakra is functioning properly, we are able to accept ourselves without conditions, and accept those around us without judgment. A closed chakra equals hatred, anger, jealousy, self-pity, paranoia, and fear. It keeps us trapped in lower consciousness. All negative emotions must be released and resolved so the heart can open up again to the higher self (nirvana).

Heart Chakra Tools

*see *Resources* on page 111

- Use a "Fitbit" to track your daily steps and goals*
- Stand up desk: standing is the new walking; it's the latest trend since fitbit!*
- Dance/movement: freedom to move fluidly in space
- Essential Oils: Juniper, Rose, Jasmine, Bergamot—with diffuser in office and home*

- Meditation Apps for guided meditations*
- Extra vitamin C to strengthen your immune system
- Music as a tool for moving from your mind and into the body: for example, simulating the feeling of sitting in a spa instead of in traffic
- Sauna: detox the body
- Be intentional with your thoughts: create focused intentions, write them down and say them out loud to attract them into your life
- Yoga poses: cobra pose, camel pose*

I love my painted chakra rocks!

Journal Entry – August 25, 2018

Last night my lower back was in so much pain. I'm standing at the sink doing dishes and suddenly the pain kicks in. So I listen to my body and lay down on the couch. I then do a few yoga poses (including happy baby) to release my back. I feel so much better than I did before!

Nutrition and Exercise— Fuel, Stress-Relief, Recovery, and Energy

"The first wealth is health."
—Ralph Waldo Emerson

Listening to Your Inner Wisdom

What and when you choose to eat affects your body, mind, and soul. We all have free will to eat whatever we want, whenever we want. However, if you eat at certain times of the day (like right before bedtime) it can negatively affect your sleeping patterns. And sleep is vitally important so that your body recovers, heals and rejuvenates itself. If you choose to eat unhealthy foods (processed foods and/or foods with a lot of sugar for example), then you may find yourself not feeling well with the resulting highs and lows— the side effects of ingesting sugar. And the more sugar you have, the more you want.

Sugar ages the body prematurely, so respect your body and health by eating fresh, whole foods whenever possible. There are certain foods that are positive pranic foods such as honey, fruits, vegetables, and nuts. Whole foods will support your body to maintain an even blood sugar level. We need to eat extremely well when we are going through stressful times. This is an opportune time to *eat for fuel, stress,* and *recovery.* There are certain herbs and foods that can counteract the stress hormone and help to remove deep belly fat caused by stress. This layer of deep fat is dangerous because it can lead to heart attacks or other illnesses and diseases.

Negative pranic foods like garlic, onions, green chiles or hot chili peppers, coffee and tea may be nervous stimulants or intoxicants. According to the science of ayurveda, garlic and onions are medicinal. As a result, you may want to limit them when you are well and eat more when you are sick. Otherwise, the body gets used to them and they cannot heal you when you need them most. If you choose to drink coffee or tea, that is fine. But if you become addicted to them and can no longer choose to drink or not drink them, they may become negative. Tap into your inner wisdom to identify which foods are good for you. *Change the way you eat by changing your focus to view food as fuel.* For instance, I know that I *love* my coffee, but I must stop drinking it by 2 p.m. in order to stay in balance and not let it negatively affect my sleep patterns.

Exercise Replenishes Your Life Force Energy

Exercise gives you more energy, which allows you to give off positive energy. *Exercise can fill us back up with vital life force energy.* Most people believe that we need extra energy in order to exercise, but in reality, the reverse is true. *We have the ability to get more energy by exercising.* I am finding that Mindful exercise is best for me. Fast, hard, strenuous exercise can cause more damage than good because it can beat up your body and your knees, for example. I have found that yoga, walking, biking, weights, and swimming are some of the best exercises for *my* body since it works my mind and body at the same time.

I love to use exercise as a tool to bring the mind and body back into balance. It creates a sense of bliss for me as I practice yoga, walk, meditate, swim or ride my bike. Doing these activities in nature adds another level of bliss for me. One of my girlfriends recently told me that she likes to swim because it is meditative. I never thought of it that way before, but now that I can see it from her perspective, it provides a meditative experience for me, too! Dancing is my favorite type of exercise because it is joyful and fun—it doesn't even feel like exercise!

Food is Medicine

Following the last few tax seasons, I have done a 7-day cleanse where I ate mostly whole fruits and vegetables. During the week (and especially once the week was over) people started asking me what I was doing differently. It was so noticeable because I felt so much better and looked like I had come back to life after the long and stressful tax season. *The food had brought me back to life.* And then, I realized that we can use food as medicine to heal our bodies.

It has been said that we should hydrate by drinking water equivalent to half our body weight in ounces each day. If you can eat whole foods and follow a healthy diet, you will be setting yourself up for success.

One of the tools I use is the **Blood Type Diet App** by Dr. Peter D'Adamo (see *Resources* on page 111). If I don't feel well after eating, I just notice what I have eaten and look it up in the blood type diet App to see if it is on my "foods to avoid" list based on my blood type. It usually is, so then I make a mental note not to eat that again. Each morning I drink warm water with lemon—it's detoxifying to the body. It also helps with elimination. Green tea is a good addition for the afternoon to support the small intestine and also protects your arteries and veins. Eating healthy can look different for everyone since our bodies need different things, so make your choices based on what your body is telling you.

Get Organized for Better Health

I make bone broth about once a week during tax season so I can have homemade chicken soup with the bone broth to support my immune system. Planning ahead by purchasing healthy foods and cooking for the week really helps me to stay on track with my eating. When you get busy and don't have time to prepare food when it's time to eat, you will tend to eat whatever is easy and available. To avoid this, it's important to plan ahead and organize your menu, shopping, and advance preparation.

Our Environment and Emotions Affect Us on a Cellular Level

Avoid steroids, pesticides and hormones: organic and fresh is best as free radicals can build up in our bodies. Anger, hostility, and resentment cause inflammation in your body. Meditation, joy, and happiness reverse inflammation.

Dr. Emoto's experiment with water (see *Resources* on page 111) shows us how the molecules change based on their environment. When we play beautiful music the water forms into beautiful crystalline shapes. On the other hand, when hateful or angry remarks are made, the water forms chaotic and ugly shapes. This shows us that everything is connected. When we bless our food and water with love, it will have healing properties for our bodies. When we talk to our flowers and plants and animals with love, they will grow and flourish. You can experiment with this yourself. Roses have the highest vibrational energy—go have a conversation with a rose!

Try this experiment:

Get two roses and talk to one with love and the other with anger. Notice what happens to each flower over the course of a few days!

Speak Your Truth

"In the attitude of silence the soul finds the path in a clearer light, and what is elusive and deceptive resolves itself into crystal clearness. Our life is a long and arduous quest after Truth."

—Mahatma Ghandi

Lately, I've been having trouble speaking up and feeling ignored or misunderstood by others. These are just a few signs of an unhealthy throat chakra. My throat has been hoarse and I have been coughing for a few weeks now. It is clear to me that I am working through some throat chakra imbalances. Essential oils, yoga, mindfulness, singing, laughing, and meditation are just some of the tools that can be used to heal it. Aletheia Luna, author of *The Ultimate Guide to Throat Chakra Healing for Complete Beginners* shares, "As a result of cleansing your throat chakra, you will experience more clarity, trust, joy, and freedom as a result of being able to communicate with confidence."

In order to be in alignment with your authentic self, you must live your Truth, and this requires that you speak up for what is important to you—a challenge for so many of us! Truth is different for everyone—your truth is yours alone. It will likely change when you can expand and see situations from different perspectives. The first step of getting into alignment with your authentic self is awareness. You need to pay attention and be the observer of your life and your experiences. Everything that is happening *"to you"* is really happening *"for you"*. It is part of your life path. You are here to learn and grow from your experiences. By observing without judgment, you can see things from a different perspective and gain clarity around a situation. If you have preconceived ideas before you go into a situation, you are judging. You must step outside the box to see things differently.

Lead with Compassion

Recently, I was in a car that was cut off by another car. The driver of the car I was in was incredulous at how someone could so rudely cut us off. I immediately reflected and then responded, "Always make generous assumptions." I explained that we must assume that the other person is going through something terrible and we don't have enough information to know all of the facts. I gave a few examples, like, "Maybe they're rushing someone to the hospital..." or "They're rushing to save their family from some emergency situation". This simple exercise brought in a different perspective. We were relieved that it had nothing to do with the driver after all.

You, too, have the ability to alchemize the stories in your mind and hold compassion in your heart. The message was loud and clear and truly enlightening! We can learn a lot through open communication and with an open heart. By truly listening and asking questions, we can learn the truth about a situation. In order to uncover the truth, we need to listen to both sides of a story and then rise above the situation to see it from a higher perspective and create a breakthrough to the truth.

Reverse Engineer Your Eating with Ayurveda

Ayurveda is a 5,000-year-old consciousness-based system of holistic health from India which integrates the mind, body, and environment. When you have balanced your health by reducing toxins in your system, you will experience more vitality. If your circulatory channels are blocked with toxic residue, your digestive power is weak, and you need to detoxify your system so that you can metabolize your food properly.

Ayurveda teaches that you can achieve and maintain a vibrant and joyful state of health by identifying your mind-body constitution and creating a lifestyle that supports your unique nature. Food is medicine!

I have studied ayurveda on and off over the past few years. There are three mind-body constitution types, or *doshas*: Vata (space and air), Pitta (fire and water) and Kapha (earth and water). There is a simple quiz you can take to discover your dosha at **http://bit.ly/366RyWw.**

"Every human being is considered a mixture of these three types with their corresponding qualities, although typically, in any one person, one or two doshas predominate...Chronic stress, which is a common aspect of modern life, can keep norepinephrine in circulation more often than necessary, chronically hindering digestion...The microbiome is a community of bacteria that live inside your digestive tract, primarily in your large intestine, or colon...our cravings, weight, and personality are controlled in part by our gut bacteria. The bad guys who are busy crowding out the good guys have, in the interests of their own survival, figured out how to manipulate the host (that's you) by sending their own signals to the brain: signals like 'Eat sugar now!' or 'We need French fries!' They do this via neurotransmitters that they produce and send to your brain."

—Kulreet Chaudhary and Eve Adamson, *The Prime: Prepare and Repair Your Body for Spontaneous Weight Loss*

The four stages of ayurveda mentioned in *The Prime* can help to detoxify and reset your body, crush cravings, and create spontaneous weight loss. I noticed that after I completed stage one, my cravings were substantially reduced. Today, my body is making adjustments—not always comfortable, but much needed. As I move on to stage two, I am excited to see the benefits it will bring to my mind, body, and soul.

The Universal Law of Resonance

This Law determines what is attracted to you based on the frequency of energy that is chosen by you through your emotional response system. Your thoughts, beliefs, and emotions activate the Law of Attraction which harmonize with energies that vibrate (or resonate) at a similar frequency. These frequencies determine and create your physical results. Think of yourself as a magnet. Whatever you are thinking and believing is what you are manifesting into your life. Abundance is everywhere. If you can slow down, focus your intentions and find inner peace, you will see it all around you. This happened to me when I was on vacation. I was meditating daily, swimming, playing and everywhere I went, I saw sacred geometry, synchronicities and so much beauty!

Throat Chakra (5th)

- "I Speak"
- Expression
- Color: blue

The throat chakra is located at the base of the neck and the color is blue. The sense is sound, the element is ether and it represents the thyroid gland. It relates to speech, hearing, and self-expression. The fifth chakra governs communication powers of all types including verbal and body. When this chakra is blocked, loss of voice or hoarseness can be the result, as well as fear of being exposed.

Luckily, we have free will and decision-making power to choose healthy foods, hydrate more, and avoid caffeine when it is not good for our bodies. We can also use natural energy boosters such as herbs, spices and essential oils that are sourced from nature and are much better alternatives than coffee and energy drinks, which leave you with caffeine crashes. Herbs, spices and essential oils contain no additives and are full of beneficial vitamins, minerals, and nutrients.

Throat Chakra Tools

*see *Resources* on page 111

- Cleanse—sample recipes*
- Recipe for Smoothie for cold*
- Yoga pose to open throat chakra: bridge pose and shoulder stand*
- Yoga poses to help your digestion: triangle, cat-cow, downward facing dog, bridge, corpse pose, lord of the fishes twisting pose*
- Essential oils: Basil, Rosemary, Spearmint*
- Lapis Lazuli stone or wear blue

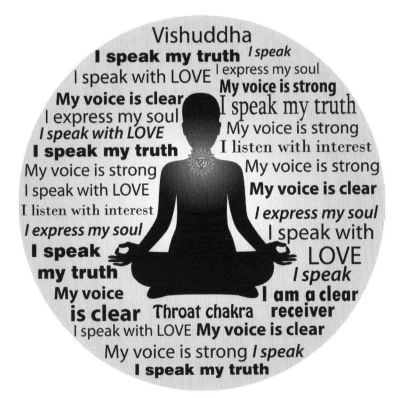

Journal Entry – November 26, 2017

I have discovered that Life Force (also known as Prana) is the key to life. I will work to harness my vitality with Life Force energy so I can stay young and vibrant!

Connect to Center

Finding Freedom

Freedom is about getting to zero. I recently studied Joe Vitale's law of attraction program and learned that you can clean and clear your energy with a Hawaiian practice of forgiveness and healing called *Ho'Oponopono*. It is comprised of four simple statements and is a simple way to set yourself up for success and freedom so that you can intentionally attract what you want into your life. The four statements are as follows (you can say them in any order you wish): "I'm sorry. Please forgive me. I love you. Thank you."

Here's how *Ho'Oponopono* works: With your old, negative limiting beliefs running on autopilot through your subconscious (and sometimes conscious) mind, you are usually unknowingly sending those signals out to the Universe. As a result, that is exactly the energy you will attract back into your life, since *like attracts like*. By practicing *Ho'Oponopono* and clearing negative thoughts and emotions, you will experience more freedom.

Zen-Like Focus

I notice that when I am doing yoga, walking, swimming, or biking, I breathe more deeply and am able to get into a deeper meditative state, which I call my *"Zen-like focus"*. We all tend to multitask these days, with so many distractions from our technology and lists of things to do. But if you can stop multitasking and focus on one thing at a time, you can actually get more done. By adding focus to what you are doing, you can more easily gather all of the facts, listen intently, and ask good questions in order to uncover the answers, or as I call it, the *Truth*.

While writing this book, I used an App called **Focus Keeper** (see *Resources* on page 111). I found that it kept me *so* focused, that after the first 25 minutes were up and I was supposed to take a 5-minute break, I wanted to keep going! I did that a few times before I took a break. The timer was a challenge for me to beat, so it was just like playing a game—and the reason I kept going. When you create challenges for yourself to get things done where you normally might procrastinate, it will motivate you to start. As the saying goes, "You can't finish what you don't start!"

Finding Peace in Chaos

By cultivating inner peace and getting into a *flow* state, we can actually get more done with less effort. Most mornings, I start my day with meditation, gratitude practice, and exercise (such as walking on my treadmill, slow flowing yoga, a walk in nature, or simply breathing deeply to get out of my head and into my body. I also do Qigong or other energy routines every morning to set myself up for success.

During the day, I will take a break by walking in nature, creating something with art, meditation, or listening to music. The goal is to meditate, draw, or create something at your desk for a break—optimally every 90 minutes at first—until it becomes a habit. At this point, it gets easier and easier to get into a *flow* state. When I walk in nature now, my body and mind connect instantly because they both know where I am going, thus making it easier to relax each time I practice it.

Pulitzer Prize nominated author Steven Kotler popularized the study of 'flow.' His books include *Bold, Rise of Superman, Stealing Fire,* and *Abundance.* In *Bold,* he describes *flow* as "moments of total absorption, when we become so focused on the task at hand that everything else falls away. Action and awareness merge. Time flies. Self vanishes. All aspects of performance—mental and physical—go through the roof."

A *flow* state allows us to get out of the detail and see things from another (higher) perspective. This allows us to understand both sides of a conflict or argument, for example. We can also see everything that is going on in a situation, just like an eagle flying overhead can see all sides of the mountain (vs. the one side we can see from the ground where we are standing). An expanded perspective allows us to make better, more informed decisions because we have more information and facts than would otherwise be available. By aligning ourselves with our center, we can get into this *flow* state quickly so that we can receive the informational downloads we need.

"Flow appears near the emotional midpoint between boredom and anxiety, in what scientists call the flow channel—the spot where the task is hard enough to make us stretch but not hard enough to make us snap. How hard is that? Answers vary, but the general thinking is about 4 percent. That's the sweet spot. If you want to trigger flow, the challenge should be 4 percent greater than the skills."

—Steven Kotler, author of *Bold*

Integrating Your Conscious and Subconscious Minds

When the conscious mind and the subconscious mind clash, you may find yourself listening only to your conscious mind. The reality is that your subconscious mind is correct more often than not, but the conscious mind is louder and may be drowning out your subconscious mind. Your conscious mind thinks in a linear fashion, is directional, and can get itself going quickly, but lacks the depth to be able to steer you to the best outcome on its own. Your subconscious mind can see in all directions (I like to think of it as an *infinity symbol*). It thinks both logically and "outside the box". When your subconscious is not in agreement with what you are consciously thinking, you will receive an emotion to let you know. Then you *feel into* the issue, you *allow your conscious mind to explore your subconscious mind* for answers and support. Listen to that little voice inside of you because not only does it organize and optimize the decisions, but it also watches over you! When we find a way to integrate the conscious and subconscious mind, we can uncover sacred wisdom and this leads to an even deeper sense of Freedom.

One day during tax season, I couldn't figure out the solution to a client question. The next morning when I was taking my longer-than-usual, well-deserved, hot shower (which I so enjoy during tax season to get me going in the morning), the answer came to me out of thin air! It amazes me how when I am relaxed and there is no pressure to figure things out, answers come so much more easily! When we use our subconscious mind, we are not blocking answers or options with our logical conscious mind.

Integrating Intellect with Intuition

We must train ourselves to *listen to our sacred wisdom,* and learn to *trust it.* We can play at a much larger bandwidth if we tap into our intuition and inner stillness and integrate it with the intellectual thinking mind. We can flow more easily with this inner knowing, rather than just staying stuck in our thinking minds, trying to figure everything out. The first step is to just get comfortable with not knowing the answer. Just be willing to sit and listen to your inner wisdom about what desires you have. Feel into what would be the most nourishing way to get something done. The masculine way is just pushing through and draining yourself until it's done. When we are so busy in our thinking minds, we cannot be attuned to our intuition. So simply slow down, put one hand on your heart and the other on your belly, and ask yourself a question you need an answer to. Your intuition is another source of intelligence to access your inner truth so you can follow the voice of your soul. It is a way to tune in and access a new neural pathway which gets stronger the more you tap into it and use it.

"We cannot solve our problems with the same thinking we used when we created them."

—Albert Einstein

Create Recess at Work

In order to create balance, it is so important to be "present" and not multi-task. Scheduling in time for sleep, exercise, meditation, focused work time, and play and hobby-time is a must. Finding leisure time is key for keeping our bodies and minds running smoothly.

Another way to get into a *flow* state is through creativity. By stepping away from your desk and focusing on being mindful and present, you can get projects done with less effort. Use your creativity to draw, paint or play to get into the *flow*. You will support your manifesting through these types of kinesthetic experiences and by allowing your soul to take the lead in the art-making process. I use colored pens and pencils, a creative and colorful notepad and colorful highlighters at work. This activates and reminds me to use my creativity and to think outside the box. I also use a tool called "mind mapping", which is very useful for activating your creativity and flow (see *Resources* on page 111).

The Power of Now

"Forget the past and live the present hour."
—Sarah Knowles Bolton

Living in the present moment is sometimes referred to as *Being in the Zone.* Eckhart Tolle explains how we can use meditation to live in the present moment. But a "true meditative state" of consciousness is not required. The present moment is usually overlooked habitually and unconsciously because our entire life *only* consists of the present moment. People live as though the present moment is disliked or hidden. The journey into the NOW is:

1. Notice your surroundings, then become aware of those sense perceptions (using the five senses).

2. Acknowledge what is.

3. Appreciate it.

The sensory perceptions that reveal the world to you get you out of your "thinking" mind and let you use your senses instead. Consciousness is continually being absorbed by thinking, amplified by our technology (we are drowning in mental thoughts and physical technology) and missing the present moment. It produces anxiety, anger, feelings of never having enough, and always needing the next thing. Your next step is to be in a state of alert awareness. Mindfulness is presence. So aim for less thinking (with alertness) and more presence and being fully here with your intention. You may also sense the fact that you are *alive* and part of the experience of the NOW—presence within and presence without. Can you feel your entire body as an anchor for being present? Because the unconscious mind is very clever, and if you don't have an anchor, the mind can come in with a thought that requires your immediate attention, and that thought will multiply into other thoughts.

CPR for Your Soul

Do you learn best by seeing it (visual), hearing it (auditory), reading/writing or by doing it (kinesthetic)?

When you discover your learning style, you will begin to understand your life in a whole new way! I am kinesthetic and have experienced that meditation using all five senses is quite helpful for me. When I focus on visualizing my breath going from my throat to my heart on the inhale and from my heart to my throat on the exhale, it stops my thinking mind. Using my essential oils to breathe in a relaxing scent helps me feel grounded and supported as well—I focus on the scent and it brings me out of any mind chatter. Try putting a drop in your hands and then rubbing them together, cupping your hands over your nose, and breathing in the scent. These practices are like CPR for your soul! It is a way to stop your thinking mind because you are focusing on what you are sensing, whether smelling, seeing, hearing, tasting, or feeling. By knowing your learning style, you can set up a routine that helps you stay present, meeting your unique needs.

Release to Receive

Another way that I have stopped the chatter is through the practice of yoga. This practice is about emptying your vessel of all the chaos and clutter in order to receive new insights and information. I find that "legs up the wall" is especially helpful. This pose can stop the chatter in your mind and has healthy side effects because inversions reverse the blood flow in your body. By releasing the chatter, you are making space for new and better ideas and insights to come to you. It is similar to releasing physical clutter and making space for new and better things to come.

Using Music as a Healing Tool

When I work late into the night during tax season, I listen to SPA music, especially on my commute home. This makes me feel like I'm flying or sailing home late at night with ease and grace. I also use my commute time to learn by listening to audible books. This makes my commute very comfortable and the time goes by quickly. An added benefit is that by the time I get home, I have shed any stress from the day and am relaxed and ready for sleep! You can also listen to your favorite songs while moving your body in dance. This allows you to get grounded and puts you in a state of joy. It also raises your vibration which sets you up to attract more good things into your life. *Chakradance* is an intuitive dance that integrates body, mind and spirit. Check out "Chakradance: Open, move, heal and balance the 7 Chakras" on YouTube at **https://youtu.be/vzrv-3ogdeg**. Use music to follow your bliss and joy!

Third Eye Chakra (6th)

- "I See"
- Connected
- Color: indigo/royal blue

The third eye chakra is associated with the fire element and represents the convergence of mind and body. Its color is indigo, and it represents the power of the mind, spiritual connection with a higher power, decision-making, and intuition (your "6th" sense). The third eye chakra is located in the center of the brow, connects to the pineal gland, and is associated with various cognitive faculties of the mind. The pineal gland produces melatonin which controls waking and sleeping cycles, our intuition, imagination, higher perspective, and clear thinking. If blocked, there can be a lack of clarity, a cloud of energy, or a confused mental state resulting in indecisiveness and irresponsibility. It is important to nurture your spiritual self and love yourself from the inside out by working with the third eye.

Third Eye Chakra Tools

- Meditation
- Creative expression
- Practice yoga
- Hang out with Friends
- Play with animals
- Be optimistic
- Get a massage
- Express gratitude

Universal Law of Correspondence

This law shows us the meaning of "As above, so below". Ultimately, life in the physical world comes into form based on your choices and perceptions in the upper, more cosmic realms. This law speaks to the manifestation of your creations in the physical, mental, and spiritual realms. So keep your mind and thoughts positive since *what you think about manifests into your physical reality*. You are a bridge and can manifest from the spiritual world to the physical world by simply focusing on your intentions, and then taking inspired action.

It is helpful to engage all five senses to experience *flow*. You can use an essential oil diffuser or bring in beautiful flowers to raise the vibration of a room. Practice yoga or energy medicine exercises to move the energy in your body and balance your chakras. You can listen to 528hz music or mantras which resonate with your body. Try the App **Insight Timer** (see *Resources* on page 111) for meditating. Color therapy is also another way to awaken our senses. Laughter is also a great way to create an endorphin release in your body. Just keep your energy level high and never use up your reserves!

Tools for Connecting to Center

- Exercise
- Qigong
- Music
- Dance
- Mantras
- Color therapy
- Laughter
- Yoga poses: easy pose, child's pose, cat/cow*
- Essential oils: geranium, lavender, rose*

Journal Entry – August 3, 2016

Last night I took a shower and got ready for bed, did the alternate nostril breathing exercise, a wonderful evening meditation using lavender oil, and did a gratitude exercise. I also changed my alarm clock to wake up at a later time than usual. Not only did I sleep well, but I also woke up on my own before my alarm went off!

Excellent Sleep

"Sleep is the best meditation."

—Dalai Lama

Sleep is Healing Medicine

Sleep is so important and rejuvenating for our bodies and minds. This is the time when our bodies heal themselves. If we do not get enough sleep, we run the risk of being susceptible to illnesses and disease. We can actually reverse illnesses and heal ourselves while we sleep. This is why when we are sick, we need to get extra sleep and bed rest. We can create rituals or routines to set ourselves up for excellent sleep.

Follow Your Circadian Rhythms

The circadian rhythm is the body's internal clock that rules the sleep cycle, hormone levels, metabolism, and other critical mechanisms of health. This biological clock is in tune with and set by natural factors like the sunrise and sunset, but it can be affected by irregular sleep patterns, the blue light emitted by your cell phone, and meal timing.

There are tips and tricks for following our circadian clock in order to maximize the flow of vital force energy. We can increase natural sunlight or bright light exposure during the day. We can simply take a morning walk if it is a sunny day outside. This activates our body and improves our energy. We can also decrease blue light exposure in the evening, which is a byproduct of television, computers, and our cell phones, for example. This blue light exposure tricks our brain into thinking that it is daytime. It reduces your melatonin hormone which helps you sleep. So avoid television and electronics in the bedroom because even after they are shut off, blue light is still being emitted into the room. Avoid using electronics right before bed because the blue light affects your ability to relax and go to sleep.

You can also decrease the amount of caffeine intake in the afternoon. I have a rule of not drinking coffee in the afternoon because I know that I will have trouble sleeping. You should also try to go to sleep and wake up at consistent times every day (including weekends) so that your body will get used to this schedule. Reduce napping during the day so that your body is ready for sleep in the evening.

There are many tools that we can use in order to sleep better including 528 hz music, an evening gratitude practice/journal, drinking chamomile tea before bed, or taking an epsom salt bath with a few drops of lavender essential oil. Avoid strenuous exercise late at night, since it will reactivate your energy which may cause restless sleep. Ensure that your bedroom is dark, quiet and at a comfortable temperature.

Our quality of sleep is so important to our health, especially as we age. A study at Iran's Kerman University of Medical Sciences shows that, "Rosemary aids in sleep and memory". In this double-blind, randomized study, 68 university students took either 500 milligrams of rosemary or a placebo each day for one month. The rate of students reporting a good night's sleep rose from 47 percent to 67 percent. (from December 2018 *Natural Awakenings*, Lee/Collier Edition).

Bedtime Gratitude Journal

By creating a gratitude practice where you journal or list three things you are grateful for each night before you go to sleep, you can actually sleep better. This exercise sets you up for excellent sleep and you can program your subconscious mind to get answers to questions you have while you sleep and dream. Be sure to write down your dreams as soon as you awaken so they don't slip away. You can sometimes see a pattern with your dreams later by reviewing your dream journal.

Listening to Your Unconscious Dreams: Your Encoded Map

There is a strong correlation between sleep and how your body functions. Your body needs quality sleep. Sleep relieves stress. It is critical for our over-all functioning. Sleep helps combat stress and heals your body and mind.

> *"Until you make the unconscious conscious,*
> *it will direct your life and you will call it fate."*
>
> —C. G. Jung

You can uncover your encoded map for your journey with various tools. There are many lenses you can look through to find the next step on your path. I liken my journey to an archaeological dig and have created a map using tools such as human design, numerology, astrology, dreams, intuition, and various other divination tools. Your subconscious mind is so powerful. Dreams can be an important part of your life. There may be messages and/or synchronicities hidden in your dreams. Your subconscious mind has messages for you, and those messages can only come through when our conscious minds are "sleeping". Your dreams can be the vehicle to show you the symmetry that occurs in your waking life.

"A dream is a small hidden door in the deepest and most intimate sanctuary of the soul, which opens up to that primeval cosmic night that was the soul, long before there was the conscious ego."

—C. G. Jung

Creating Your Vision

You must have a vision for yourself to manifest what you want into your reality. What do you want to BE? Dream it into BEING using your feelings (how will you feel once you have it, what will it look like, see as many details as possible). Once you know what you want, you can set GOALS. Then you can take small steps daily towards the goals. If you don't know what you want, take small steps to try different things until you find something that you are passionate about. You can use the Lighthouse Method.

Making Change with the Lighthouse Method

The lighthouse method can be used when you aren't sure what you want. Maybe you are feeling stuck somewhere in your life (your career, relationship, or in general) and don't know how to get out of it.

"If you want to make a life change but have no idea what it should be, think of that change as a lighthouse far away. You know neither what the lighthouse looks like nor its location. You can only see its dim, distant light. To reach it, you need to step offshore, point your boat in the direction of the light, and row... Moving a stopped boat requires will and energy. It's easier to keep moving by rowing small, consistent strokes."

—Stacy Kim, "How to Make a Big Change", Real Simple Magazine, January 2018

Many of us will try to plan everything out *before* taking any action (this is the perfectionist in us) which results in *never* taking any action since we don't know where we are going. And this leads to feeling "stuck" in the mud and unable to move forward!

With the lighthouse method, you take small action steps in a direction, try different ideas and see what resonates with you, putting you in the flow and bringing you joy and bliss. You can redirect as you discover what does not bring you joy. Once you find something that clicks, follow your bliss which then creates purpose and passion in your life. Keep up momentum with small steps and break down big projects into smaller steps. This method will also bring you abundance when you discover your passion because you are in a state of joy when you are doing it. Be the change you want to see in the world!

Universal Law of Divine Oneness

Quantum physics shows us that everything that exists is connected to everything else, and that we are all *One*. Everything we think, do, and say has an effect on others and on the entire world around us. We are connected to everything in nature and in the universe. The way we treat others mirrors back how we get treated by others, like a ripple effect. It is important to be kind with our thoughts, actions, and our words. Words can impact others more than we realize— remember Dr. Masaro Emoto's water experiment?

Crown Chakra (7th)

- "I am Divine"
- Know
- Color: violet

Our crown chakra is violet (also seen as white or gold) and is located at the top of our head. It represents the pituitary gland and spiritual connection or enlightenment. It goes beyond the elements and senses and represents our connection to supreme consciousness. It is our detachment from ego and the gateway to heaven. When this chakra is closed, the mind is closed and you won't listen to reason or allow any other opinions. In order to experience higher consciousness, one must have an open mind. Having a blocked crown chakra can also obstruct your ability to release materialistic needs.

Crown Chakra Tools

*see *Resources* on page 111

- Yoga poses: corpse pose (savasana), headstand*
- Gratitude journal
- Dream journal
- Meridian Health Clock App*
- Music
- Essential oils: Geranium, Lavender, Rose, Clary Sage, Sandalwood, Jasmine, Vetiver, Cedarwood, Frankincense*

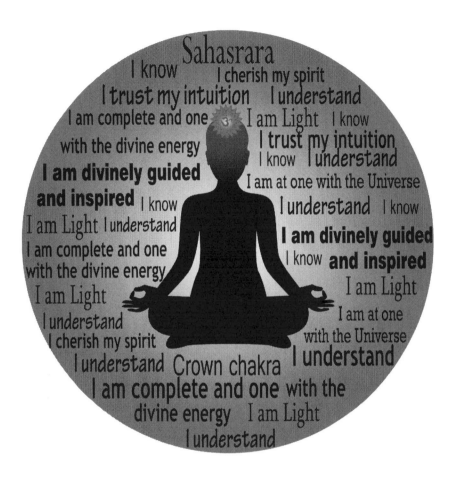

Unlocking Wealth and Freedom

No matter how much money you have, certain blocks may can keep you from experiencing your full earning potential, as well as keep you trapped in the cycle of debt and money struggles. Trapped emotions in your physical body can cause all types of problems, including mental blocks that have been stored in your subconscious mind, as well as physical illnesses.

In the book *The Emotion Code*, author Bradley Nelson talks about how releasing these trapped emotions through muscle testing (such as the sway test and the use of magnets) brings a new joy and freedom to your life. It can bring a new balance and inner calm to your being where nothing has helped before. By releasing the trapped emotions, tapping into joy becomes easier.

Once you open yourself to what brings you joy (other than what money can buy you), then you start to shift out of scarcity consciousness and into true prosperity consciousness.

This is the key to earning more, saving more, and spending your money wisely. Once you are no longer trapped in scarcity consciousness, money becomes a source of hope, confidence, and joy.

"It has nothing to do with manifesting millions and everything to do with knowing how to open, give, receive, and serve the Flow."

—Tosha Silver, author of "It's Not Your Money"

Your psychological patterns and trapped emotions can create money blocks that end up getting in the way of creating success in your business.

These trapped emotions can stem back to how you grew up with money, a significant event you experienced later in life, or some unknown loyalty, among other reasons. The pain and heightened responses from the trapped emotions can create pain and sadness in your body.

When you break free from scarcity beliefs and blocks by releasing trapped emotional energy from the physical body, you will attract money in your business, whether it is by solving a problem, having clarity around your compelling message, or asking for the sale. Your new frequency will allow you to attract the money you need and build your business.

Money is energy and loves movement and your attention. So pay attention to money and do not ignore it! If you are presented with opportunities and intuitive insights about how to grow your money but you don't take action, the opportunity will move on to someone else. Notice any patterns that arise when you pay attention to what you say to yourself when you handle money (paying bills, receiving money, shopping or dealing with clients who say *no*, for example) and when you ignore it. Once you can establish a good relationship with money, it will reward you and flow to you more easily in your business.

What will make you happier? What are your values? We can measure if we are on target by comparing your top few highest spending categories to see if they are in alignment with your values.

The Root of Your WealthFlow Code is Linked to Your Dharma

In Buddhism, "Dharma" means "cosmic law and order". Once you discover your Dharma and uncover your gifts, you can align with them and live a more authentic life. Your purpose may change over time as you evolve in your life, but your shift into alignment with your authenticity and inner power will bring you prosperity—which includes not just wealth, but good health, love and communication, community support, joy and happiness, inner peace, and financial support.

You came here to do meaningful work by being in service to others and sharing your gifts with the rest of the world. Now, you can unlock the key to your freedom by finding your truth and embracing your calling. When you are hiding or living your life to make other people happy, you are not in alignment with your design and it is much more difficult to find happiness.

Creating Your Mind Map

Creating a mind map is a great way to manifest your dreams and desires. To do this, start in the middle of a page with a goal you would like to achieve. Then create a map with any ideas to reach that goal around the center linked by curvy (not linear) lines to inspire more flow and creativity. It is similar to a vision board, but more amplified as you connect your vibration to the frequency of what you want to attract. Then, you can map out a plan to reach the goal for the first 90 days (quarter) and get it onto your calendar. Add this mind-mapping exercise to your daily meditation and gratitude practice to transform your dreams into your three-dimensional reality.

Here are some Sacred Prosperity Goals you can add to your Mind Map:

- Pay down debt
- Have a budget
- Spend less than you earn
- Invest for your future
- Negotiate for everything
- Give back to your community—give to receive
- Align your spending with your values and goals

Living Deliberately with Playful Joy

Find your inner freedom through discipline, focus, and depth of experience. Create adventures in your life! You must *feel* into the sensations of adventure. Before I go to Florida on vacation, I can already feel the warm sunshine, smell the fresh clean air, hear the birds singing, and see and hear the beautiful ocean. I can even taste the fresh vegetables from the farmer's market because I know this adventure well! You too can create adventures that are near and dear to your heart and experience them through visualization and use of your senses—even when you're not there yet!

Surround yourself with plants and let the sunlight in. The reverberations around us from our technology, air conditioners, and machinery are making us ill. We need to spend more time in nature! We are becoming less and less active as technology becomes more and more prevalent. The amount of physical activity we are performing is so low that our systems are getting out of balance. When we feel that we are getting sick, we must jump into activity and do it with joy and do more of it, because the moment we go back, we are empowering the illness. Activity is a simple solution for everything. Just do something *joyful*—go play or dance! Run around and be in joy and feel your aliveness. Your fundamental problem is that you have become too serious about your life. Loosen your grip, drop the rope, and enjoy life a little so the last scene can be different!

Dance to teach your body to be spontaneous, respond to your intuition and to move into change quickly and effectively instead of running away. Dance raises your vibration.

Decide to have a life that supports you in the creative ways you dream about.

Commit to what it is that you want to create. Don't procrastinate. Whatever you resist most, do that first to get it out of the way! It makes you really creative and inspired. Otherwise, we spend so much time resisting what we don't want to do. It uses up our power and is an energy leak, like a hole in a tire. It silently drains you until you finally do it anyways but from a place of depletion.

Allow yourself to align with your true self and begin to live more authentically! Live your legacy by aligning with your "inner" resources to generate energy, self-love, self-worth, and own your value. By focusing more inwardly versus externally through activities like meditation, yoga, walking in nature, or practicing mindfulness, you will be inspired to shift from your mind to your heart and then to your solar plexus (where your soul connection or universal energy resides). You must make the choice to take the chance if you want anything in your life to change. In his article "7 Tips to Make a Positive Change in Your Life" John Rampton says, "If you want to make a change in your life, you can do so positively by following these seven tips:

1. Identify and understand what you want to change

2. Rid your life of negativity

3. Exercise more often (Just Do It!)

4. Be kind to others

5. Build a support network

6. Eliminate the nonessentials (visual and emotional clutter)

7. Take baby steps

Break the big picture goal down into systematic, manageable baby steps. Then document and celebrate your wins daily.

"Life shrinks or EXPANDS in proportion to one's courage."

—Anais Nin

Keep your thoughts positive and focus on *joy*. Joy is a state of *being*. Follow your bliss. When you are in a state of Joy, you create abundance because you are attracting that same Joy to you. Life is not *happening* to you, it is *responding* to you. This is your path to Freedom! You can open a portal to a new paradigm because being-ness is the beginning of all prosperity. If you are doing something because you love it, you are showering everything with joy and people will pay you for who you are. The money you earn has nothing to do with the hours you work—it has everything to do with the amount of *joy* you feel. All you have to do is bring your energy into harmony with money. You cannot harmonize with money if you think it's evil. Remember the Law of Attraction, where "energy attracts like energy." The question is always "How do I feel?" If it's not joyful, don't move in that direction. The way to achieve peace and happiness is to start a business making *joy*, rather than making money.

Joy is the ultimate money magnet and secret formula to success and financial flow.

In the book *The Abundance Code*, Julie Ann Cairns writes that if your conscious desires are not in alignment with your subconscious beliefs, you cannot manifest what you want into your life. This is called "subconscious sabotage" or "a formula for frustration." She explains that most of us have inherited several core limiting beliefs about money that are actually *stopping* us from attaining wealth—no matter how much we may want that abundance or how hard we may be working toward getting it. She calls these limiting beliefs the "7 Money Myths". These beliefs are passed down from generation to generation and are the mental programs that hold us back from experiencing a life of abundant wealth and freedom. Cairns goes on to say that we can update our mental software system and overwrite our subconscious poor programs with a much better alternative: our *Abundance Code*.

"There is no path to happiness. Happiness is the path."

—Gautama Buddha

There are several techniques you can you use to release negative beliefs about money that will allow you to attract more wealth into your life. You have certain patterns that are running behind the scenes in your subconscious that may be sabotaging you... but you *can* shift your subconscious mind programming!

Emotional Freedom Technique (EFT), also known as Tapping, is a popular method that uses the fingertips to tap on acupuncture points while emotionally tuning in to negative attitudes and past experiences, thereby clearing these inner blocks.

In her book *Tapping into Wealth*, Margaret Lynch explains how to Tap to clear any inner blocks to attracting and managing your wealth: "It wasn't until I discovered EFT Tapping that everything changed for me. It was at that moment that I began to realize that what I had always thought was an 'outer game'—working harder, getting lucky breaks, the economy—was really much more of an 'inner game,' as were my perceptions, decisions, belief systems, traumas, and more."

Another technique is *ThetaHealing*—a process of meditation created by Vianna Stibal in 1995. Wikipedia states, "Practitioners claim ThetaHealing teaches people to develop natural intuition through changing their brain wave cycle to the theta waves with the intention of exploring how emotional energy affects a person's health."

In *Theta Healing: Introducing an Extraordinary Energy Healing Modality* author Vianna Stibal shares, "One of the things that you must remember when you are working with the subconscious mind is that you have to use words that the subconscious understands. One of the concepts that the subconscious mind does not understand is the word 'try'. You cannot *try* to do anything. You either do it or you don't do it." To learn more, read *Sisterhood of the Mindful Goddess* by Windy Cook and Julie McAfee.

By changing your words and thoughts, you have the power to change your life.

To create change in your life, you must change how you think about things. Shift from negative thinking to intentional thinking. Become the observer of your thoughts. Train yourself to notice any negative thoughts that are disempowering you. When they appear, say "Cancel and clear that thought!" Thoughts are so powerful—what you think is who you are. Your perception is your reality, and your thoughts create your world. So shift your thinking to bring more joy and abundance into your life.

In *Conscious Luck: Eight Secrets to Intentionally Change Your Fortune,* Gay Hendricks and Carol Kline recommend removing underlying unconscious blocks because we have been conditioned by other people's opinions and thoughts about what we should be doing. It's time to release the social conditioning and any shame you may be holding onto. Instead, choose to transform your shame into a magnet of abundance!

Conclusion

The Art of Balance

Breathe deeply! The key to life is *perfecting the art of balance* between the polarities that exist in our world. By integrating the practices and tools of the WealthFlow Code into your life, you will experience an unfolding process resulting in joy, inner peace, and a sense of trust and faith.

Simplify your life. Focus on transforming *any* self-criticism into self-compassion. You are the observer of your life, not the judge!

Gratitude invites you to explore yourself and the world around you—it attracts success! Through a daily gratitude practice, you will cultivate the power of deep appreciation so that it becomes your way of life.

Get present and catch yourself in any story such as "When I...then I'll". Instead, change your focus to create the results you want.

Acting "As If" Helps You Manifest

Be grateful for what you already have, and act *"as if"* you already have what you want. Balance depends on making constant adjustments to the ego—basically, getting out of your head and into your heart more often!

"The longer you linger in gratitude, the more you draw your new life to you."

—Dr. Joe Dispenza

Be mindful and stay present in the moment. Instead of living life from the perspective of *have-do-be*, let's flip it to *be-do-have!* Embody who you desire to *be*, then you will *have* the things you want and need by attracting them into your life. The best balance happens if you can *be* while you are *doing*. Action is required. As the saying goes, "When you pray, move your feet." We must take action.

> *"We are not human beings trying to be spiritual.*
> *We are spiritual beings trying to be human."*

As we come to the end of this journey together, I want to leave you with the acronym "BALANCE"—an easy way to remember and practice the WealthFlow Code 7-step system and keep your chakras balanced. Note the first letter of each word spells out "BALANCE".

1. **B**reathe

2. **A**sk for Support

3. **L**isten to Your Body

4. **A**ccept Yourself

5. **N**utrition and Exercise

6. **C**onnect to Center

7. **E**xcellent Sleep

I encourage you to practice using these 7 steps of the WealthFlow Code so you can create more BALANCE in your life!

Now, go back to the beginning of this book and start again. Move through this information with patience and leave plenty of room to read and integrate the practices.

I believe in you! You can unlock your gifts, elevate your life, and create the change you desire. You are not alone as you step into the next best version of YOU.

~Namaste

Julianne

Resources

INTRODUCTION

doTERRA® Essential Oils
Visit my site for wholesale prices on your essential oils!
https://www.doterra.com/US/en/site/juliannejoy

STEP 1: JUST BREATHE

Calm App
https://apps.apple.com/us/app/calm/id571800810

Circle of Life Assessment
https://www.mindtools.com/; www.wheeloflife.noomii.com

doTERRA® Essential Oils
https://www.doterra.com/US/en/site/juliannejoy

Focus Keeper App
https://juliannejoy.me/wealthflowcodegifts

Grounding Meditation
https://juliannejoy.me/wealthflowcodegifts

Isaac M. O'Bannon, editor of CPA Practice Advisor
https://www.cpapracticeadvisor.com/contact-us/
contact/10270140/isaac-m-obannon

Meridian Health Clock App
https://apps.apple.com/us/app/meridian-health-clock/
id424591129

Root Chakra Meditation
https://juliannejoy.me/wealthflowcodegifts

Sacred Powers by Davidji
https://www.amazon.com/dp/1401952836

Synctuition App
https://apps.apple.com/us/app/synctuition-meditation-program/id1166940722

STEP 2: ASK FOR SUPPORT—NOTIFY AND EDUCATE YOUR NETWORK

doTERRA® Essential Oils
https://www.doterra.com/US/en/site/juliannejoy

Focus Keeper App
https://juliannejoy.me/wealthflowcodegifts

Yoga poses for stress relief and excellent sleep
https://juliannejoy.me/wealthflowcodegifts

STEP 3: LISTEN TO YOUR BODY AND PRACTICE EXTREME SELF-CARE

doTERRA® Essential Oils
https://www.doterra.com/US/en/site/juliannejoy

Gabrielle Roth's 5Rhythms movement meditation
https://www.youtube.com/watch?v=uyhs2mNLgyA

Yoga poses for stress relief and excellent sleep
https://juliannejoy.me/wealthflowcodegifts

STEP 4: ACCEPT MYSELF—"I CONNECT TO THE NEEDS OF MY BODY"

Calm App
https://apps.apple.com/us/app/calm/id571800810

doTERRA® Essential Oils
https://www.doterra.com/US/en/site/juliannejoy

Fitbit
www.fitbit.com

Insight Timer App
https://apps.apple.com/us/app/insight-timer-meditation-app/id337472899

Synctuition App
https://apps.apple.com/us/app/synctuition-meditation-program/id1166940722

Trauma Release Exercise (TRE)
https://traumaprevention.com/

Yoga poses for stress relief and excellent sleep
https://juliannejoy.me/wealthflowcodegifts

STEP 5: NUTRITION AND EXERCISE—FUEL, STRESS-RELIEF, RECOVERY, AND ENERGY

Blood Type Diet® by D'Adamo Personalized Nutrition
https://apps.apple.com/us/app/blood-type-diet/id379485721

Cleanse—Sample Recipes
https://juliannejoy.me/wealthflowcodegifts

Cold-Busting Pineapple Smoothie Recipe
https://www.littlesugarsnaps.com/2015/01/06/

Dosha Quiz
http://bit.ly/366RyWw

doTERRA® Essential Oils
https://www.doterra.com/US/en/site/juliannejoy

Dr. Emoto's experiment with water
https://youtu.be/5cyQVu_8EFc

Yoga pose to open throat chakra: bridge pose and shoulder stand; Yoga poses to help your digestion: triangle, cat-cow, downward facing dog, bridge, corpse pose, lord of the fishes twisting pose; Yoga poses for stress relief and excellent sleep:
https://juliannejoy.me/wealthflowcodegifts

STEP 6: CONNECT TO CENTER

Calm App
https://apps.apple.com/us/app/calm/id571800810

doTERRA® Essential Oils:
https://www.doterra.com/US/en/site/juliannejoy

Focus Keeper App
https://apps.apple.com/us/app/focus-keeper-time-management/id867374917

Insight Timer App
https://apps.apple.com/us/app/insight-timer-meditation-app/id337472899

Mind Mapping exercises
https://www.mindmapping.com/

Synctuition App
https://apps.apple.com/us/app/synctuition-meditation-program/id116694072

Yoga poses: easy pose, child's pose, cat/cow
https://juliannejoy.me/wealthflowcodegifts

STEP 7: EXCELLENT SLEEP

doTERRA® Essential Oils
https://www.doterra.com/US/en/site/juliannejoy

Human Design
https://www.jovianarchive.com/get_your_chart

Meridian Health Clock App
https://apps.apple.com/us/app/meridian-health-clock/id424591129

Numerology
https://www.thelawofattraction.com/what-is-numerology/
https://cafeastrology.com/

Yoga poses for excellent sleep
https://juliannejoy.me/wealthflowcodegifts

UNLOCKING WEALTH AND FREEDOM

The Emotion Code, by Bradley Nelson
https://www.amazon.com/dp/1250214505

CONCLUSION

Tapping into Wealth: How Emotional Freedom Techniques (EFT) Can Help by Margaret M. Lynch and Daylle Deanna Schwartz M.S.
https://www.amazon.com/Tapping-Into-Wealth-Emotional-Techniques/dp/0399168826

About the Author

Author **Julianne Joy** is certified in Reiki 1, Law of Attraction, and Numerology.

She also serves as a Certified Public Accountant (CPA) and partner at Simione Macca & Larrow LLP. Throughout her 30+ year career, she has built her practice based on the foundation of relationships and serves her clients with the ultimate goal of seeking to do what is best for each client.

Julianne graduated from the University of Connecticut with a Bachelor of Science degree in Accounting and has provided accounting, auditing, consulting, and tax services to a wide variety of industries, including clients in architecture, engineering, construction, real estate, insurance, manufacturing, printing, and not-for-profit.

In addition to her work in accounting and auditing, Julianne advocates for her clients by supporting them with tax planning and projections and guiding them through tax audit representation with the Internal Revenue Service and State of Connecticut. She has also assisted clients with financial reporting, accounting and cost controls, systems, business planning, mergers and acquisitions, financing, and cash flow analysis, playing a critical role by acting as a catalyst for her clients to navigate their businesses, especially through times of change.

She is also a member of the American Institute of Certified Public Accountants and the Connecticut Society of Certified Public Accountants, where she served on several committees over the years including the Federal Tax, Community Service, and Continuing Education Committees. She served a three-year term as a member of the National PCPS Technical Issues Committee, which monitors technical issues and developments in accounting, auditing, professional ethics, peer review, and governmental accounting that could have significant effect on closely held companies, not-for-profit organizations, government, and the CPAs who service them. She also served on the Professional Issues Task Force. Julianne enjoys collaborating and networking with the expanding world marketplace through MSI Global Alliance, an international network of more than 250 legal and accounting firm connections in more than 100 countries.

A founding member of Women's Wellness Fund at Middlesex Hospital, Julianne is actively involved in the Women's Business Alliance of Middlesex Chamber. She enjoys giving back to the community by being actively involved in causes close to her heart through volunteer opportunities that support animals, the environment, and healthcare.

Julianne is a contributing author to two books in the best-selling New Feminine Evolutionary Series, also published by Flower of Life Press:

Set Sail: Shine Your Radiance, Activate Your Ascension, Ignite Your Income, Live Your Legacy—"10 Ways to Cultivate Resilience, So You Can Flow with Change" and *Practice: Wisdom from the Downward Dog*—"Yoga: A Pathway to Inner Peace". *The WealthFlow Code* is Julianne's first solo book.

Most of all, Julianne enjoys writing and spending time with her family and Chinese crested dog, Isadora.

For your FREE audio download of Julianne's "WealthFlow Code Meditation" plus additional bonuses, visit **www.JulianneJoy.me**

·······⚮·······

Additional books by Flower of Life Press

The New Feminine Evolutionary: Embody Presence—Become the Change

Pioneering the Path to Prosperity: Discover the Power of True Wealth and Abundance

Sacred Body Wisdom: Igniting the Flame of Our Divine Humanity

Set Sail: Shine Your Radiance, Activate Your Ascension, Ignite Your Income, Live Your Legacy

Practice: Wisdom from the Downward Dog

Sisterhood of the Mindful Goddess: How to Remove Obstacles, Activate Your Gifts, and Become Your Own Superhero

Path of the Priestess: Discover Your Divine Purpose

Sacred Call of the Ancient Priestess: Birthing a New Feminine Archetype

Rise Above: Free Your Mind One Brushstroke at a Time

Menopause Mavens: Master the Mystery of Menopause

The Power of Essential Oils: Create Positive Transformation in Your Well-Being, Business, and Life

Self-Made Wellionaire: Get Off Your Ass(et), Reclaim Your Health, and Feel Like a Million Bucks

Emerge: 7 Steps to Transformation (No matter what life throws at you!)

Oms From the Mat: Breathe, Move, and Awaken to the Power of Yoga

Oms From the Heart: Open Your Heart to the Power of Yoga

The Four Tenets of Love: Open, Activate, and Inspire Your Life's Path

The Fire-Driven Life: Ignite the Fire of Self-Worth, Health, and Happiness with a Plant-Based Diet

Becoming Enough: A Heroine's Journey to the Already Perfect Self

The Caregiving Journey: Information. Guidance. Inspiration.

Plant-based Vegan & Gluten-free Cooking with Essential Oils

www.floweroflifepress.com

FREE TRAINING: www.bestsellerpriestess.com/bestseller-priestess

Made in the USA
Middletown, DE
02 October 2020